THE ART OF THE INTERIOR

TIMELESS DESIGNS BY THE MASTER DECORATORS

Acknowledgments

It is impossible to express our gratitude to all those who have collaborated on this volume and who have trusted in us. However, Sophy Thompson and Kate Mascaro from Flammarion deserve a special mention, for believing in our project from the outset.
We also thank the author of the foreword, the *éminence grise* of American interior design John Saladino, who commented on our approach to the art of decoration with his usual perceptive insight.
Our thoughts are especially with those who are no longer with us—Billy Baldwin, Madeleine Castaing, Bill Willis, Emile Targhetta d'Audiffret de Gréoux, Dennis Severs, and Andrée Putman—whose exceptional creations continue to delight us.

Photography: René Stoeltie
Text and Styling: Barbara Stoeltie
Translated from the French by Elizabeth Heard
Design: Barbara and René Stoeltie
Copyediting: Susan Schneider
Typesetting: Cyprien Godin
Proofreading: Nicole Foster
Color Separation: IGS, L'Isle d'Espagnac, France
Printed in Singapore by Tien Wah Press

Simultaneously published in French as *Intérieurs de Louis XV à Andrée Putman*
© Flammarion. S.A., Paris, 2013

English-language edition
© Flammarion, S.A., Paris, 2013

ISBN: 978-2-08-020140-9

Dépôt légal: 09/2013

BARBARA & RENÉ STOELTIE

THE ART OF THE INTERIOR

TIMELESS DESIGNS BY THE MASTER DECORATORS

Foreword by John Saladino

Flammarion

Contents

Foreword

Interior design, when undertaken by people with great talent, becomes fine art. The complex effort to orchestrate a room in three dimensions is always biographical. Environments, rooms—or however you wish to name a space that has been professionally conceived and executed—are the personal reflection of the occupants' emotional identity. Starting from Imhotept's great Egyptian burial vaults, the journey through time conjures up beautiful rooms either designed for or by the powerful and the artistic. I can only imagine Cleopatra's large, propagandistic and feminine sleeping chamber. Hadrian's multicolored marble retreat and Caravaggio's iconic red and ebony studio, slashed by an array of gold light like his paintings, are great temples of personal history. Moving through the Renaissance and the Rococo, Marie-Antoinette's refreshing attempt at restraint, or Mozart's rooms furnished in perfect scale to match his music, we discover within the pages of this book the major influences in the work of many designers and decorators.

The finest rooms that both embrace us and inspire us are seen here in this lavishly photographed compendium of professional endeavor by Barbara and René Stoeltie. This is a book that Cole Porter would have had in his New York penthouse library.

—John Saladino

Introduction

We all have a deep-seated desire to beautify our homes, however modest they may be. From the beginning of time, we have experienced an irresistible urge to create a comfortable shelter that enhances our quality of life.

At the dawn of human civilization, *Homo sapiens* readily exchanged a bed of twigs and dry leaves laid out beneath a starry sky for the reassuring safety of a deep cavern. Within these dark caves, our Neanderthal and Cro-Magnon forebears strove to find protection from storms and the unrelenting threat of predators. It is no longer a surprise that our early ancestors longed to adorn their primitive dwelling places, covering the walls and vaults of their troglodyte havens with hunting scenes. Since their discovery in 1940, the Lascaux Cave frescoes have astonished the most discerning eye with their timeless beauty.

When the English archeologist Howard Carter excavated the tomb of Pharaoh Tutankhamun, he was the first to peer into the royal chamber through a breach in the wall. His simple utterance, proclaiming that he saw "wonderful things,"[1] is indelibly recorded in history. Before Carter's marveling eyes lay an astonishing spectacle: he saw a magnificent array of furnishings and objects, tangible proof that the citizens of that extraordinary ancient civilization possessed an unmatched aesthetic sensibility. They had satisfied their deep-seated yearning for the rare and the beautiful by creating sumptuous dwellings, decorated with magnificent furnishings and works of art.

For centuries, curious crowds have thronged the thoroughfares of Pompeii and Herculaneum and scoured Greece in a quest for vestiges of the cradle of our civilization. We rhapsodize over the ruins of patrician dwellings decorated with frescoes and swoon over the classic beauty of the temples and sculptures of ancient Greece. But as we marvel over the neoclassical architecture of a Parisian *hôtel particulier* built during the reign of Louis XVI, or admire an eighteenth-century English manor in a secluded park by the renowned landscape architect Capability Brown, we often travel through time without pausing to consider the geniuses responsible for these impressive structures and their interior decoration. Who was the first man—or the first woman—to contemplate a plan for the murals of the House of the Vettii in Pompeii or to adorn the great hall of a medieval castle keep with a tapestry depicting an imaginary garden? Who first drove back the gloomy shadows that permeated majestic Renaissance palaces with an abundance of chandeliers, candelabra, and *torchères*? Who were the first artists to carve *boiseries* with elaborate scrolls and rocailles to grace the walls of innumerable French châteaux, putting their own distinctive mark on the styles that were named after the monarchs of the time?

Today, the words "decorator" and "designer" are part of our everyday vocabulary. When the French refer to an attic room tucked beneath the eaves as a *mansarde*, few are aware that it owes its name to the architect who created the Château of Versailles. We describe a piece of furniture as "Louis XV," referring to the dates of a French king's reign. If an interior seems almost too refined or feminine, we might mention the Marquise de Pompadour, the mistress of Louis XV, who was renowned for her elegance and taste, without giving the allusion much thought.

Madame de Pompadour, Madame du Barry.... We should not forget that before their gentle aesthetic despotism, which ordained the presence of Sèvres bisque porcelain and François Boucher's rosy nymphs, interior decoration was primarily the domain of men. William III of England and his wife Mary Stuart II confided all responsibility for decorating their castles to the French Huguenot architect Daniel Marot, who published books with samples of ornamental motifs that can still be seen today on the historic facades and interiors of Amsterdam and The Hague.

The geniuses of neoclassicism in England and Germany went by the names of Robert Adam and Friedrich von Erdmannsdorff. We cannot imagine a facade or interior of a British castle or the contemporary German *Schloss* that does not draw on that architectural vocabulary of tympanums, columns, pilasters, niches, cartouches, and medallions.

In the early nineteenth century, their disciple was Karl-Friedrich Schinkel. His palaces, bridges, summer residences, public buildings, and churches still miraculously grace Berlin, a city that has been repeatedly scourged by war. He did not confine himself to innovative architectural designs, but also directed his talents to embellishing gardens and interiors. It is entertaining to speculate what he would have thought had he lived long enough to see the ornamental excesses and strange cocktails of historical styles concocted during the reign of Napoleon III. Suppose he had been the guest of the Duchess of Uzès at her château in La Celle-les-Bordes; she blithely covered the walls of this vast hunting lodge with nearly two thousand hunting trophies fashioned from the heads of stags and does (technically referred to by the grisly term *massacres*) that she had killed by her own hand.

Curiously, it was a short time after the reign of Napoleon III and Empress Eugénie that the concept of a "decorator," as we know it today, first emerged. Jan-Hendrik Jansen moved down to Paris from his native Dutch town of Amersfoort. He changed the Netherlandish cadences of his name to Jean-Henri, set up shop on the rue Royale, and met with immediate success when he offered his decorating and interior design services to Paris's upper crust. The era favored decorative excess, with overstuffed chairs, lavish window treatments that resembled theater curtains, and hybrid styles such as Louis XVI Impératrice, overloaded with heavy passementerie trim and palm trees. Furniture imitated the elaborate inlays of the seventeenth-century cabinetmaker André-Charles Boulle, and these pieces were as welcome in the reception rooms of wealthy bankers as they were in the boudoirs of the courtesans known as *les grandes horizontales*. After such visual over-indulgence and ostentatious faux luxury, it comes as no surprise that, toward the end of the nineteenth century, there was a movement that abruptly turned its back on pastiches of the past. Enough of the overdone Henri II look and fussy Marie-Antoinette-style furniture made popular by the reigning queens of theater such as Hortense Schneider and Sarah Bernhardt. This new movement, called "Art Nouveau" after the name of Samuel Bing's emporium, was led by Victor Horta, Henry Van de Velde, and Charles Rennie Mackintosh (although the last had a profound dislike of Belgian and French Art Nouveau). They were three giants in a movement that was to overturn architectural and decorative conventions, whose remarkable innovations proclaimed the advent of industrial design.

And what of women? What was their role in the art of decoration? Not all were content to docilely fulfill the role of housewives; some had the audacity to elbow their way onto the stage and demonstrate their own talent for defining good taste in a business dominated by men. They followed the examples of style arbiters Edith Wharton and Elsie de Wolfe. It was a time when ladies of high society or from the cosseted bourgeoisie began to attract attention: they had just as many bold and original ideas as their male counterparts. The early twentieth century saw the debut of the woman decorator, the woman architect, and the woman designer. Madeleine Castaing rose to prominence, although she was a young woman from a rigidly bourgeois background that swore by the ponderous Louis XV and Louis XVI styles. Throughout her career (and her long life), Madeleine Castaing, who became a professional decorator at a fairly advanced age, put her mark on an era and introduced a style that still bears her name. It is a style characterized by the recurrent, and even obsessive, use of leopard-patterned carpeting, nineteenth-century mahogany furniture, and opaline lamps and vases in a range of acidulated candy colors. This surprising but happy marriage gave rise to a totally re-imagined nineteenth-century style that was revisited by this decorating genius.

Is the decorator a man or a woman? With the dawn of the twenty-first century, the art of interior decoration pays no heed to the sex of anyone who can raise the common-place chore of selecting a sofa or window treatment to the level of an art form. Originality and inventiveness are all that matter, along with the intense pleasure of a custom-designed dream space. Anything goes—"Mix and match," Zen-like serenity, or a meticulous reproduction of period decor. We might recall a few lines penned by the witty hand of the celebrated journalist and novelist Louise de Vilmorin: "Our homes are our prisons. Let us try to regain our freedom in the way we decorate them."[2]

1. Howard Carter, quoted in: Nicholas Reeves, John H. Taylor, *Howard Carter before Tutankhamun* (London: British Museum, 1992), p. 141.
2. Louise de Vilmorin, quoted in: Barbara Stoeltie, *Rooms to Remember* (London: Frances Lincoln, 1998), p. 13.

A Nordic "Folly"

Daniel Marot

Daniel Marot was born in Paris in 1661 and grew up during the reign of Louis XIV. His father was none other than Jean Marot, the architect and engraver for His Majesty's court. Young Daniel learned his trade from his father and André Le Nôtre, the king's landscape architect. At a very young age, he was entrusted with the task of documenting contemporary architecture and engraving plates showing historic events.

One of those historic events was to alter the course of Marot's life. In 1685, Louis XIV signed the revocation of the Edict of Nantes. Like many other Huguenots, Marot no longer felt safe in his native country and fled to the Netherlands, where exiled Protestants were welcomed with open arms. He moved to The Hague, and his presence immediately came to the attention of the *stadhouder* and Prince of Orange-Nassau, William III. When William became King of England, Ireland, and Scotland in 1689, he asked Marot to accompany him to his new realm.

When we think of Marot, we think of Hampton Court, the palace and gardens of Het Loo, the facades and interiors of an impressive number of patrician dwellings in The Hague and Amsterdam, and, above all, his elegant, exuberant style. His characteristic generously proportioned scrolls are abundant in his furnishings and decorative objects. Marot's distinctive look became known as the "William and Mary style," and it pervaded the decor of the era with its vast canopy beds luxuriously draped with silk damask, its mantelpieces lavishly decorated with corbels and Chinese porcelain, and its gardens *à la française*, richly planted with colorful parterres. After the death of William III in 1702, Marot returned to the Netherlands and continued to embellish aristocratic

homes and castles belonging to the nobility of his adopted country. Regrettably, the work of Marot, who died in 1752, has not come down to us intact. Although many of his interior designs can still be seen in their original state, very little remains of the gardens and follies he designed. Rosendael Castle, located in the eastern part of the Netherlands in the county of Gueldres, is a happy exception.

In 1714, fire destroyed a large portion of the castle, and the new owner Lubbert Adolf Torck decided to raze most of the medieval section, while keeping the donjon intact. Against this medieval structure, he built a charming house in the neoclassical spirit. It is unclear when he decided to commission Marot to decorate the park with a shell gallery, a cascade, and an octagonal pavilion. Today, we can take delight in the beauty of these additions, marveling over the parterre peopled with statues concealing trick fountains that spray unwary visitors, and the white marble cascade guarded by tritons and dolphins.

Rosendael's octagonal pavilion, a very exceptional feature, is sometimes eclipsed by other follies and passes unnoticed, despite its abundance of decorative elements typical of Marot's distinctive style. This compact little building, designed primarily as a resting place for strollers in the park, for intimate meals and—who knows? —for the occasional romantic tryst, features paneling painted in various delicate shades of blue, wall consoles, gilded mirrors, and a white marble serving table, all testifying to the love of luxury that was shared by Marot and his patron alike. In a setting such as this, one comment suffices: *"Que la fête commence!"* (Let the celebration begin!).

*

13, 14–15: The terrace has a grotto adorned with shells and a pair of classical goddesses. 16: In the octagonal tea pavilion, Marot's paneled walls are hung with mirrors and consoles. 17: In the center of the octagon stands a table arrayed with period Delft faience, shells, fruits, and a stuffed peacock. 18: A statue of a triton ornaments the cascade carved from white Carrara marble.

A Masterpiece of Bavarian Rococo

François de Cuvilliés

Labeling the rooms in the elaborate hunting lodge of Amalienburg is largely irrelevant. No one ever cooked a single morsel in the kitchen that is covered from floor to ceiling with Delft faience tiles; the roof terrace served no purpose other than as a perch from which the prince and his guests could take aim at pheasants. Although they were remote from this unconventional way of life, the contemporaries of Amalienburg's architect, François de Cuvilliés the Elder, considered this pavilion in the grounds of the Nymphenburg Palace near Munich to be a masterpiece of Bavarian rococo.

François de Cuvilliés was born in 1695 in Soignies, a small town in the Belgian province of Hainaut. He was scrawny and very short. The Prince Elector Maximilian Emmanuel of Bavaria, who had pleasure-loving courts in both Brussels and Mons, made him the court dwarf. De Cuvilliés followed his master on his wanderings through Paris, Namur, Compiègne, and Saint-Cloud. After the Treaty of Rastatt ending the War of the Spanish Succession was signed in 1714 they proceeded to Munich. There, thanks to his remarkable artistic gifts, he became the official architect of the Bavarian court of the Prince Elector Charles VII.

From 1720 until 1724, de Cuvilliés was sent to Paris to study the Regency style, which had become preeminent during the regency of Philippe d'Orléans. Returning to Munich, he played a decisive role in determining the new style of the Bavarian court and drew up the plans for Augustusburg Castle in Brühl near Cologne, Falkenlust Castle, and the sumptuous interiors of the Residenz in Munich.

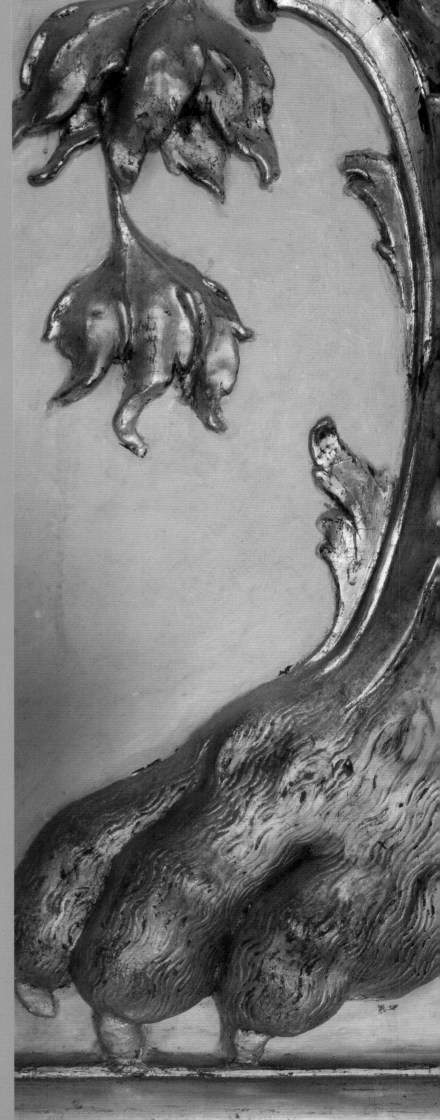

De Cuvilliés's style achieved a high point with the theater in the Residenz in Munich, which was completed in 1755. However, the rococo jewel that he built between 1734 and 1739 for Charles Albert and his wife Maria-Amelia of Austria is unquestionably the finest example of his exuberant style.

Amalienburg is tucked away in the midst of the garden of the same name, part of the vast grounds of the Nymphenburg Palace. The structure is a single-story building whose exterior gives no hint of the riotous explosion of rococo ornament within. The central part is a rotunda lined with tall mirrors, with walls painted in pale blue and a color known as "aurora," a soft shade of yellow very fashionable at the time. The stuccowork, glazed with silver leaf, is the work of the sculptors Johann Baptist Zimmermann and Joachim Dietrich. In the wings extending on either side of the rotunda are the princess's bedroom, the Pheasant Room, the Hunting Room, the kennels, the kitchen, and, with a nod to bodily necessities, a water closet.

At the time the hunting lodge was built, François de Cuvilliés took up drawing again. In 1754, he published a series of engravings of elaborate motifs that provides a flawless document of his vision of the rococo. Both flora and fauna inspired his ornamentation in Amalienburg; the interior seems to have been invaded by an exuberant multitude of flower garlands, branches, and hunting trophies. Lofty French doors allow daylight to flood the interior, and enormous reflecting panels in the Hall of Mirrors replicate the trees and park into infinity.

Francois de Cuvilliés died in Munich in 1768. With him passed the era of the exuberant rococo, and its riotous scrolls and arabesques.

*

21: In the bedroom of Maria-Amelia of Austria the paneling is the purest rococo style. The silk damask bed coverings and the paneling are both "aurora" yellow. **22–23:** Stuccowork with silver-leaf ornamentation. **24:** Paintings of the Flemish and French schools, set into the paneling and surrounded with arabesques and motifs featuring grotesque masks.

Le Roi S'Amuse

Georg Wenzeslaus von Knobelsdorff

Eccentric, intelligent, with an omnivorous appetite for culture; crafty, cruel, ill-tempered, and malicious; an aesthete, musician, soldier *extraordinaire*, and above all King of Prussia—Frederick II (better known as Frederick the Great) was an extraordinary figure. Traumatized at an early age by a sadistic father who had his son's best friend, Hans Hermann von Katte, executed for high treason before the boy's very eyes, the young Frederick finally began to breathe freely with his accession to the throne in 1740. A close friend and patron of Voltaire with a fascination for everything French, a poet in his spare time, composer of over one hundred sonatas, a flute concerto, and a number of military marches—all of genuine merit—this king despite himself, a monarch without peer, was also a passionate aficionado of architecture. The palaces he built in Berlin and his domain in Potsdam are among the most significant masterpieces of the Prussian rococo.

In 1745, the king, exasperated by the rigid protocol of the court in Berlin, longed to retreat to a summer palace near the capital from early April to the end of October. He asked the architect Georg Wenzeslaus von Knobelsdorff (1699–1753) to build him a summer residence on a hill overlooking the park of the royal domain in Potsdam, presenting the architect with designs he had drawn himself.

Von Knobelsdorff, an erstwhile soldier turned professional architect, had an unbounded admiration for Palladio's work and the French baroque. He successfully executed the king's design by creating a one-story oblong building with just ten rooms and an imposing rotunda, overlooking a terraced vineyard. This "little house" was christened

Sanssouci—without cares—because Frederick hoped it would prove to be a retreat from wearisome affairs of state.

The Sanssouci that emerged from von Knobelsdorff's creative imagination is an intimate little château that is very far removed from the splendors of Versailles. An approaching visitor discovers an elegant structure, crowned by a dome and further embellished by a yellow-painted facade ornamented with caryatids. It is clear that the architect wished to create a residence that was closer in spirit to a luxurious stage set than a hulking colossus. After all, Frederick only used the palace for entertaining close friends, including his companion Voltaire, with whom he had a sometimes thorny relationship. Conversations during meals—which were relatively infrequent—were conducted exclusively in French. When the spirit moved him, the king would sometimes take the flutist's part during intimate concerts.

The decor of the château's interior draws inspiration from nature. In the famous bedroom, the paneling, painted chamomile yellow, is covered with garlands, little monkeys, and exotic birds sculpted by Johann August Nahl and Johann Christian Hoppenhaupt the Younger, who was responsible for the overall decorative scheme. The other rooms are equally light-spirited, without being feminine. The king imported silkworms that fed on the mulberry trees he planted in the park and produced the silk required to cover the Sanssouci furniture.

The king oversaw every aspect of his little palace in Potsdam. He selected the decoration for the porcelain, closely monitored the work of the cabinetmakers, wood sculptors, bronze and stucco workers, and painters, and insisted on the frequent use of green, his favorite color. When he arrived at dusk in a carriage from Berlin, he ordered the servants to light every crystal chandelier, as well as all the château's torches and candles.

The king dismissed von Knobelsdorff for unknown reasons in 1746, and von Knobelsdorff's colleague Johann Baumann took over the work. Frederick became an eccentric recluse who called everyone *"Mein Kind"*—my child—and wandered around the château attired in a threadbare old military uniform. He died in his bedroom in Sanssouci on August 17, 1786. In 1991, his remains were re-interred beneath a memorial stone set into the terrace of his favorite residence. Frederick the Great has returned home at last.

27: The rotunda of Sanssouci. **28:** In the small gallery, the king hung paintings of bucolic subjects by Antoine Watteau, Nicolas Lancret, and Jean-Baptiste Pater. **29:** The third guestroom, decorated by Johann Christian Hoppenhaupt the Younger. Five of the paintings on the walls bear von Knobelsdorff's signature. **30:** The silk damask used to upholster a pair of rococo armchairs also covers the walls of the salon. **31:** Frederick II himself detested silk damask. The restoration of the Sanssouci armchairs reflects the taste for luxurious silks of his successor, Frederick William. **32:** In one of the niches in the *Marmorsaal*, a statue of Venus Urania by François Gaspard Adam.

Chinoiserie in Potsdam
Johann Gottfried Büring

Hungry for diversion, weary of rigid protocol, virtual prisoners in their castles and palaces, the crowned heads of seventeenth- and eighteenth-century Europe sought out new surroundings. They scattered whimsical follies across their domains and pursued exoticism with cultish devotion. Inspired by distant lands that were generally known to their architects only through travelers' accounts with engraved illustrations, these monarchs created the private Disneylands of their time, filling their royal parks with imaginative fancies in the forms of pyramids, mock Greek temples, Turkish motifs, and Chinoiserie more elaborate than the original sources of inspiration.

Born in 1723, the German architect Johann Gottfried Büring was initially confined to a single location: the royal domain and city of Potsdam. The son of the court cabinetmaker, and a student of the painter and copper engraver Constantin Friedrich Blesendorf, he was raised to the rank of *Kondukteur* at a very young age during the construction of the terraces of Sanssouci, Frederick the Great's summer palace. After an educational tour of Italy and France, Büring moved to Hamburg. In 1754, the king ordered him to join the famous architectural studio known as the Bau-Comptoir, located in a wing of the royal residence in Potsdam, to work on beautifying the town and the royal domains.

The young architect had a remarkable gift for creating illusions; Frederick the Great, never lacking original ideas, asked him to enhance houses of no real architectural distinction with grandiose Palladian facades. Büring also built the spectacular Bildergalerie (picture gallery) for his monarch and the Neues Palais (New Palace) in the

domain of Potsdam, where he again proved his mastery of illusionism by covering the stucco facade with trompe l'oeil red bricks. Finally, he was the author of the distinct rococo style associated with Frederick the Great that culminated in the Chinese Pavilion built between 1754 and 1757; it represents the apogee of the late Prussian baroque. The pavilion in Potsdam may not be the most grandiose of the exotic pavilions built for European monarchs, but it is certainly the most enchanting. The king provided several sketches to Büring with a trefoil floor plan, directly inspired by Le Trèfle, an oriental pavilion built twenty years earlier in Lunéville by the architect Emmanuel Héré for Stanislas Leszczyński, the former King of Poland, who was living in exile in France.

In any case, the *Chinesische Teehaus* in Potsdam is a veritable feast for the eyes, thanks to the contribution of the sculptors Kambly, Heymüller, Benckert, and Giese, and the painter Thomas Huber, who designed the rotunda's ceiling and painted exotic scenes of incomparable charm. Even today, visitors have to restrain themselves from reaching up to touch the life-size, gilded Chinese figures and sandstone palms. A Mandarin gentleman with a parasol perched on top of the roof seems to cast an amused glance over the throngs below, all captivated by the king's tearoom.

Frederick the Great, a canny old fellow, uncovered irregularities in Büring's accounts. The architect was put under house arrest but managed to escape to Saxony. After Frederick's death, he requested a pardon from his successor Frederick William II, but he never saw Potsdam again. He died without honor, an inglorious end for a spinner of glorious dreams.

✳

35: The figures and stylized palm trees in the Chinese Tea Pavilion are made of gilded sandstone. **36–37:** Within the pavilion's niches, life-size statues of musicians sport exotic costumes and hairstyles. **38–39:** The rotunda's cupola with exotic scenes of people, flowers, and animals. **40–41:** Huber was primarily known for his portraits; his striking talent is evident in his rendering of figures in the frescoes. **42:** An allegory of life's pleasures in a fairytale setting: above one of the doors, a Mandarin gentleman pours himself a drink.

To Please a Prince

Friedrich von Erdmannsdorff

Enhancing the natural landscape—such was the ambition of the German prince Leopold III Frederick Franz, Duke of Anhalt-Dessau (also known as Prince Franz), when he decided to transform his domain in Wörlitz into an enchanting park. He was inspired by Jean-Jacques Rousseau's notion of a return to nature and his didactic novel *Emile*. It was to be a park filled with little islands, rivers, lakes, bridges, follies, with a neoclassical castle modeled after a great English country house.

The prince was born in Dessau in 1740. Following the finest traditions of his forebears, he was destined to serve in the Prussian army and contribute generously to the war chests of His Majesty Frederick the Great. As a young man, the prince, who was a dedicated pacifist and philanthropist, had the audacity to inform the monarch that he would henceforth devote his fortune to more humanitarian and aesthetic goals. Accompanied by his friend, the architect Friedrich Wilhelm von Erdmannsdorff (1736–1800), he launched himself twice on a cultural grand tour, visiting Italy, Holland, England, France, and Switzerland. In the course of this lengthy journey, he met prominent figures of the neoclassical movement, including Johann Joachim Winckelmann, Charles Louis Clérisseau, and Piranesi. Returning to Dessau, their imaginations brimming with ideas, the prince and his architect set to work.

Wörlitz Castle was built between 1769 and 1773 in the purest Palladian style, inspired by the elegant classicism of the Scottish architects Robert and James Adam. With its Greek tympanum, sturdy columns crowned with Corinthian capitals, and

niches containing statues in the classical style, it inspired a new generation of architects and influenced another giant of architecture, Karl Friedrich Schinkel.

This imposing structure, which overlooks a *parc à l'anglaise* from its lofty terrace, is on a surprisingly human scale. The prince lived there with his wife as if inhabiting a large country house. Indeed, this castle, evocative of a Greek temple, crowned with a charming belvedere, was designed as a summer palace where the princely couple would live only during the warmer months of the year. Despite the large reception room with its magnificent frescoes and the dining room with its colonnade and niche that holds a large collection of black basalt vases by Wedgwood, the ambiance is intimate, thanks to the graceful proportions created by the architect.

Von Erdmannsdorff was a perfectionist with a taste for the purest form of neoclassicism. The castle's interior was designed with elegant simplicity. We need only observe the spartan furnishings of the king's bedroom and the grisaille rotunda at the entrance to perceive the restrained grace of his style.

Wörlitz was opened to the public upon its completion, and the prince continued to embellish his domain with additional structures, including a Gothic house, a Pantheon, a temple dedicated to Venus, and even a lake with an artificial volcano that was crowned with an exact replica of Lord Hamilton's casino (or summerhouse) in Naples, the future Villa Emma. An impressive number of tourists visit the castle today. They invariably succumb to the charms of this artful creation that reflects a man whose dream was simply to enhance the landscape's natural beauty.

✳

45: A plaster copy of the Venus Urania, cast in the eighteenth century by the Torrenti workshops in Rome, in the entrance. 46: In Princess Louisa's bedroom, the alcove bed is set on a platform. The bust on the console is by Bartolomeo Cavaceppi. It represents Julia Sabina, wife of Emperor Hadrian. 47: Floral themes are ubiquitous in the wall decoration and also appear on the console adorned with grapevines. 48–49: In the formal dining room, von Erdmannsdorff designed an alcove for the wine cooler. The chairs are in the Chippendale style, and the classical vases on the mantel top are from the Wedgwood manufactory. 50–51: A marble statue of the young Bacchus appears to preside over the wine cooler. The grisaille trompe l'oeil painting above the fireplace is inspired by classical Rome. 52–53: In the park of Wörlitz, the prince built a number of follies. In his copy of the Villa Emma, the marble fireplace is decorated with ceramic Wedgwood inlays. The marble busts on either side of the fireplace, attributed to Cavaceppi, represent Melpomene and the Eros of Centocelle. 54–55: Engravings set into the paneling, marquetery parquet crafted from rare woods, ceilings decorated in the Pompeian style: the villa is bursting with opulent details. 56: The walls of the Chinese room are covered with hand-painted panels. The shape of the lanterns is Chinese-inspired, and the ceiling is painted with stars and a crescent moon.

The Transformation of
a Fortified Castle

Robert Adam

In 1744, Sir Thomas Kennedy, the Ninth Earl of Cassillis, inherited the fortified castle of Culzean. He immediately embarked upon a thorough restoration of the castle and added a wing on the rocky headland. But it was his successor and brother David Kennedy who brought in the celebrated Scottish architect Robert Adam (1728–92) in 1777, asking him to mastermind the castle's complete transformation.

At that time, Robert Adam was at the height of his fame, and was best known for the neoclassical buildings he had designed in England. The Adam style was synonymous with the Greek and Etruscan Revival. The artistic idiom featured columns, tympanums, Palladian windows, and lavishly decorated ceilings with motifs rendered in a palette of pastel tones dominated by pistachio green, soft pink, and pale blue. Adam considered interior decor to be just as important as the facades of his buildings, and he willingly designed furniture, mantelpieces, lighting fixtures, and carpets. Adam's involvement in Culzean Castle was ultimately somewhat limited, but by adding a spacious room to either side of the castle's central section and building an impressive new oval staircase in what had been an interior courtyard, he left an indelible mark on the structure. The existing towers were enlarged to make them more prominent and accentuate the fortress's romantic aspect. However, Culzean's true masterpiece is the decoration of the saloon in the formidable Drum Tower.

The saloon is the culmination of the Adam style, and it requires little imagination to evoke the vision of sumptuous balls and receptions set within these pale green walls, with gilded chairs and sconces, and fine examples of the Dutch School signed by

Melchior d'Hondecoeter, Jan Spruyt, and Joost Cornelisz Droochsloot. Sadly, Robert Adam died before Culzean's decoration was completed. We will never be able to see all of the elegant, extraordinarily refined finishing touches he might have added to the inner sanctum of the Kennedys' fiefdom.

In 1945, Culzean Castle was donated to the National Trust for Scotland by one of Kennedy's descendants, the Fifth Marquis of Ailsa. This distinguished organization, which has been responsible for the rescue and maintenance of so many important Scottish buildings, has created a National Guest Flat in the upper story. It served as guest quarters for Dwight D. Eisenhower on several occasions, as well as for guests of the Scottish government and distinguished visitors. The charm of the Adam style remains unmarred by the passage of time. The beauty of the neoclassical work created by this remarkable architect and decorator continues to captivate aficionados of timeless design.

*

59: In 1968, the discovery of a watercolor by Robert Adam showed that the saloon's white ceiling had originally been painted in a typically Adamesque range of pastels. **60–61:** In the saloon, which was intended for important receptions, the gilt chairs are Sheraton and the armchairs covered with Beauvais tapestry are French, dating from the reign of Louis XVI. The painting above the mantelpiece is by Deschamps, and the panel over the door is by Jan Spruyt. **62:** In the Picture Room, the Irish George II chairs are covered with petit point needlework by the Duke of Wellington's mother. The nineteenth-century harp is signed by Érard. **63:** Lord Cassillis's bedroom was restored in 1977 and the Chinoiserie wallpaper is a copy of a period design. The canopy bed is Chippendale. **64:** In the Blue Drawing Room, the silk damask that covered the walls was replaced in 1976 with a replica woven by the Gainsborough Silk Weaving Company. The mirror above the mantelpiece is a reproduction made in 1977 based on a drawing by Adam. **65:** A portrait of Napoleon Bonaparte painted in 1813 by Robert Lefèvre presides over the Best Bedroom. The bed and its hangings are in the Hepplewhite style. **66:** The space now occupied by the Oval Staircase was formerly an interior courtyard. Adam used Corinthian columns for the *piano nobile* and Ionic columns for the upper floor.

In the Footsteps of the Ancients

Karl Friedrich Schinkel

Strolling around modern East Berlin, the visitor encounters numerous neoclassical structures built by the man known in Germany as "the architect of Prussia," Karl Friedrich Schinkel. They include the Neue Wache (New Guard House), the theater in the Gendarmenmarkt Square, the bridge of the former royal castle, and the Altes Museum.

Karl Friedrich Schinkel was born in 1781 in Neuruppin, a small town in the Margraviate of Brandenburg. Having first taken courses in design from the celebrated architects David and Friedrich Gilly, the young Karl Friedrich decided that he wished to be a painter instead. However, when he encountered the mystical works of Caspar David Friedrich, Schinkel realized he could never attain such a degree of mastery and changed direction entirely. From that moment, he launched his architectural career and went on to build a series of structures that made Berlin one of the most impressive cities of the era.

Schinkel's career would not have prospered without the unwavering support of the Prussian government and the immediately enthusiastic reception by aristocratic patrons and crowned heads. Their commissions flooded in, and in less than two decades, Schinkel built a palace for Prince Augustus, a castle in Tegel, and the palaces of the princes Karl and Albrecht. The Bauakademie (architectural academy), generally considered to be his masterpiece, is a restrained structure located across from the royal palace, built of red brick and decorated with terra-cotta bas-reliefs.

The two greatest sources of inspiration for Schinkel were ancient Greece and the German Gothic style. In Berlin, he built the neo-Gothic church of Friedrichswerder, and in Rosenau he took on the restoration and decoration of the castle, giving it a medieval air. However, the genuine Schinkel style, as we understand it today, is associated with the neoclassical beauty of Berlin's Glienicke Casino and the ensemble of structures in the palace of Charlottenhof, in the heart of the royal park in Potsdam.

Karl Friedrich Schinkel was a universal genius like Leonardo de Vinci, Michelangelo, and Goethe. Whether in architecture, furnishings, decorative objects, lighting fixtures, cast iron garden furniture, or porcelain, his tireless imagination gave birth to some of the finest artistic creations of the mid-nineteenth century. His design for the palace of the Queen of the Night in *The Magic Flute* remains a classic whose loveliness has not been dimmed by time. Tragically an extended period of illness followed a cerebral hemorrhage. His premature death in 1841 prevented him from carrying out his magisterial project for the construction of a palace on the Acropolis in Athens and a castle in Orianda in the Crimea. At least we have a majestic legacy in stone that testifies to a formidable talent with an inimitable, timeless style.

*

69: In Charlottenhof's Roman baths, the walls are decorated with trompe l'oeil paintings inspired by the wall decor found in Pompeii and Herculaneum. **70–71:** In the *Gartensaal*, Charlottenhof's pavilion, a paper-mache crimson curtain inspired by theatrical sets and surmounted by a starry sky forms a backdrop for depictions of Ganymede and David. **72:** The head of Goliath, a detail of the marble statue of David that stands in a niche in the *Gartensaal*. **73:** In the crown princess's small study, the doors are covered with silver leaf. The decor of palmettes and the paneling painted with Pompeian scenes is typical of Schinkel's work. **74:** Statues of Bacchus and Apollo flank the opening to the impluvium. **75:** In Tegel Castle, Biedermeier furniture graces the Blue Room. **76–77:** Schinkel had the walls in Tegel painted with faux marble to emphasize the interior's museum-like setting. **78–79:** In the castle in Rosenau, Schinkel indulged his passion for the Gothic. **80:** In one of the bedrooms, the walls have a trompe l'oeil painting of a gazebo covered with climbing foliage.

An Equestrienne's Hunting Lodge
The Duchess of Uzès

The peaceful village of La Celle-les-Bordes lies in the département of Yvelines, close to the castle that once belonged to the formidable Anne de Rochechouart de Mortemart, Duchess of Uzès, an accomplished horsewoman and matchless huntress, who would have made Diana, the mythical Roman goddess of the chase, feel inadequate.

Anne de Mortemart, the great-granddaughter of Barbe-Nicole Clicquot-Ponsardin, who was none other than the Veuve Clicquot of the legendary *maison de champagne*, was born in 1847. She became a duchess in 1867 through her marriage to Emmanuel de Crussol d'Uzès, who purchased the château in La Celle-les-Bordes in 1870. It was a sturdy structure in the Louis XIII style, built in 1610 by Charles de Harville, and the Duc de Crussol made it the center for his hunt, known as the Rallye Bonnelles. The duke and his wife were passionate aficionados of the chase, and it is impossible to gauge which of them was the more enthusiastic. In 1880, two years after her husband's untimely death, the duchess took up the reins of the hunting company and made the Rallye Bonnelles into the premier hunt in France.

Anne de Mortemart's life was marked by an extraordinary variety of victories and defeats. A loyal Orléaniste, as devotees of the royalist cause were known, she lost a substantial part of her fortune—three million francs of the day—financing the political schemes of General Boulanger to restore the monarchy. On May 4, 1897, she had a miraculous escape from the dreadful fire at the Bazar de la Charité that claimed the lives of 129 victims. The Duchess of Uzès was indeed an extraordinary woman! Riding sidesaddle, she bagged almost two thousand deer; she was the first woman in France to

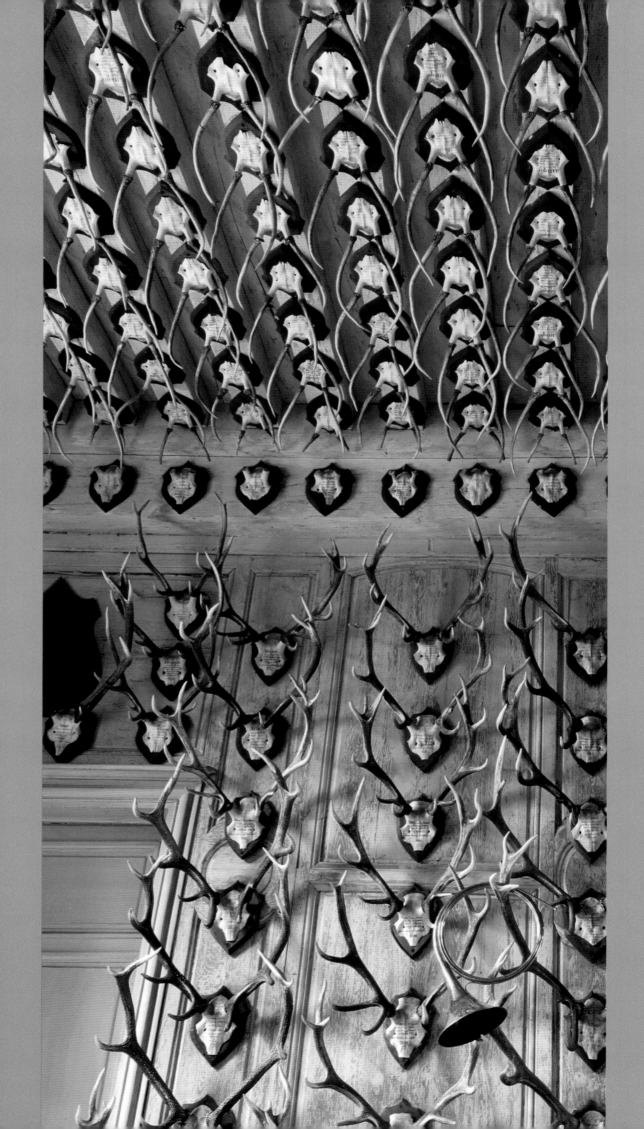

obtain a driver's license (and the first to be fined for speeding); and she later developed a close friendship with the anarchist and liberal socialist Louise Michel. A visitor to her hunting lodge soon realizes that she was far from being a commonplace personality.

In the salons of the château in La Celle, the eye is irresistibly drawn to the paneling and coffered ceilings that are bedecked with 2,400 souvenirs of the hunt. This horde of stags' antlers clearly merits the technical French hunting term for such a trophy: a *massacre*. Mounted row upon row, antlers culled from deer of all sizes and ages completely cover the wall space, leaving scarcely any room for a few ancestral portraits and providing a distraction from some very fine period furniture. The spectacle is so overwhelming that it is easy to ignore the fact that this decorative scheme was orchestrated by a woman who wanted to be surrounded with the plunder from her hunting forays, while others of her sex and rank fantasized about decorating their homes with fashionable colors and new curtains.

Unfortunately, we do not have photographic records dating back to the period when she began to mount the antlers. Presumably, the duchess selected the finest examples gleaned from each hunt, handing them over to her taxidermist. Relentlessly, more and more sets of antlers covered the walls and ceilings of the rooms. Like any collection, the one in this château possesses a unique piece that dominates all the others: a pair of heads from two stags whose antlers became entangled during a fight and were delivered from their agony by the duchess.

Anne de Mortemart, Duchess of Uzès, died in 1933 in her château in Dampierre-en-Yvelines. Lucid and vigorous to the end, this extraordinary huntress, who sported a tricorn hat with inimitable style, bequeathed her children a motto that was as tantalizing as it was mysterious: "One must be observant" ("Il faut être observant").[1] She had been exactly that throughout her life, and the outcome of this singular gift of observation is preserved today in the château that was once her hunting lodge.

---

1. Author's conversations with the Duke of Brissac, former owner of the château in La Celle-les-Bordes.

*

83: A nineteenth-century terra-cotta statue representing the infant Moses saved from the waters. 84–85: The *boiseries* of the grand salon are covered with the duchess's trophies. The wing sofa is Louis XIII. 86: The trophies of the mistress of the house also occupy the coffered ceilings. 87: The dining room. 88: A very handsome nineteenth-century canopy bed in the duchess's room.

25, Rue Américaine

Victor Horta

Born in Ghent in 1861, Victor Horta experienced a very difficult youth and adolescence. He rebelled against the authoritarian restrictions imposed by his young mother, who demanded that he pursue a career in medicine or law. His much older father (he was sixty-six when Victor was born) could barely support his twelve children with the meager income earned from his shoemaker's trade. Expelled by several schools, the young reprobate finally became interested in the art of building when he visited a worksite managed by an entrepreneurial uncle. His exasperated parents later sent him to Paris for an apprenticeship under the interior decorator Jules Dubuysson.

In Paris, Horta was fascinated equally by impressionist painting and newly introduced construction materials such as steel and glass. When his father died in 1880, he decided to return to Belgium and enroll in the Académie des Beaux-Arts in Brussels, where he became friends with Paul Hankar, was awarded a gold medal, and became assistant to his professor, Alphonse Balat. Together they designed the royal greenhouses in Laeken.

When exactly did Horta renounce upright vertical lines for sinuous contours? In 1892, he drew up the plans for Eugène Autrique's private residence in Brussels. In 1893, he built the Hôtel Tassel, with its monumental staircase whose walls are adorned with floral motifs; this building was to be considered the founding work of Art Nouveau. It is well known that the architect boasted that he "ignored the leaf and flower and only kept the stem."[1] And it is indeed that biomorphic stem, fashioned from cast iron or steel, that undulates like the tendrils of a vine around the handrail in the entrance of the Hôtel

Frison, and runs along the balcony of the Hôtel Solvay. It also wound through the vast ballroom of the Maison de Peuple, commissioned by the Belgian Worker's Party, in forms reminiscent of an enormous ribcage.

As is often the case for architects, Horta was able to give free rein to his imagination when the building was his own private residence. In 1898, as in our own time, the houses that lined either side of the rue Américaine reflected the individuality of the typical Belgian and his horror of architectural monotony. Victor Horta's *hôtel particulier* consists of two buildings with interior communication; he designed them as effectively independent structures. The private wing on the left and the atelier on the right were given completely different facades. Once inside the house, the visitor discovers a structure that is not divided into conventional stories; the main staircase opens into space, climbing progressively toward the living room, the dining room, and the upper floors with an almost total absence of walls; at the top, a large glass roof provides a source of light that illuminates the center of the house.

Victor Horta's private residence is the most spectacular of all his creations. The glass roof reflected into infinity by an array of mirrors, a radiator transformed into a column that serves as a structural support, tile-covered walls, an undulating banister, a palette of warm colors, the use of exotic woods, and furniture that Horta designed himself—all combine to create a rarefied aesthetic sensibility, unique of its kind. It is difficult to believe that this monument of Art Nouveau receded into oblivion after Horta's death and, judged as outmoded and without artistic merit, came close to being razed. It was only saved at the last moment by the action of one of Horta's former students, the architect Jean Delhaye.

Victor Horta died in Brussels in a house of no particular architectural distinction in the rue Saint-Bernard. Shortly before his death, he had emptied his attic and disposed of a mountain of old papers. Sadly, his archives and a number of other masterpieces went the way of the demolished Maison du Peuple and are now lost to us forever.

---

1. Victor Horta, quoted in: Françoise Dierkens-Aubry, Jos Vandenbreeden, *Art Nouveau in België* (Brussels: Lannoo, 1994), p. 55.

91: At the top of the stairwell, the glass roof is reflected into infinity by a mirror shaped like a butterfly's wing. **92:** The sitting room on the second floor opens onto the garden and was added in 1906. The furniture designed by the architect is made from maple and sycamore wood. **93:** In the dining room, the ceilings are arched in the form of a basket handle and the walls are covered with glazed white brick. The plaster bas-reliefs are by Pierre-Jean Braecke, and the furniture is made of American ash. **94:** In the dining room, the "fireplace" consists of a radiator topped with a display cabinet. The lighting fixtures bear the architect's signature. **95–96:** The base of the staircase is made of mahogany, and the arabesques forming the balustrade are made of cast iron strips that have been riveted and gilded.

The House on a Hill

Charles Rennie Mackintosh

In 1893, an indignant young architect convened a conference in the Glasgow School of Art and fiercely admonished his audience that it was absurd to dress up banks and churches as if they were Greek temples. There was little applause in the room: young Charles Rennie Mackintosh, who had just concluded his studies at the city's architectural academy, had the reputation of being an iconoclast who was vehemently opposed to "neo" revivalist styles, as well as to the then emerging European Art Nouveau scene that had originated in France and Belgium, which he scornfully described as being "like melted margarine."[1]

Mackintosh had a real passion for Japanese prints, as did the MacDonald sisters, Margaret and Frances, who were given to drawing highly stylized, spectral female figures inspired by the art of the Far East. With the decadent English artist Aubrey Beardsley, they organized a group known as "The Four," which was soon rechristened "The Spook School" by their critics. Despite opposition, Mackintosh's reputation spread rapidly in Europe, since his designs for the Glasgow School of Art and the interior and furnishings of Miss Cranston's new Willow Tea Rooms in Sauchiehall Street won him an invitation to exhibit at the eighth exhibition of the Viennese Succession.

Mackintosh married Margaret MacDonald in 1900. When the couple (who habitually dressed in white) moved to Main Street in Glasgow, they jointly designed an entirely white interior with white furniture that attracted the attention of the Scottish publisher Walter Blackie, who had just purchased land in the hills of Helensburgh, a small fishing village west of Glasgow.

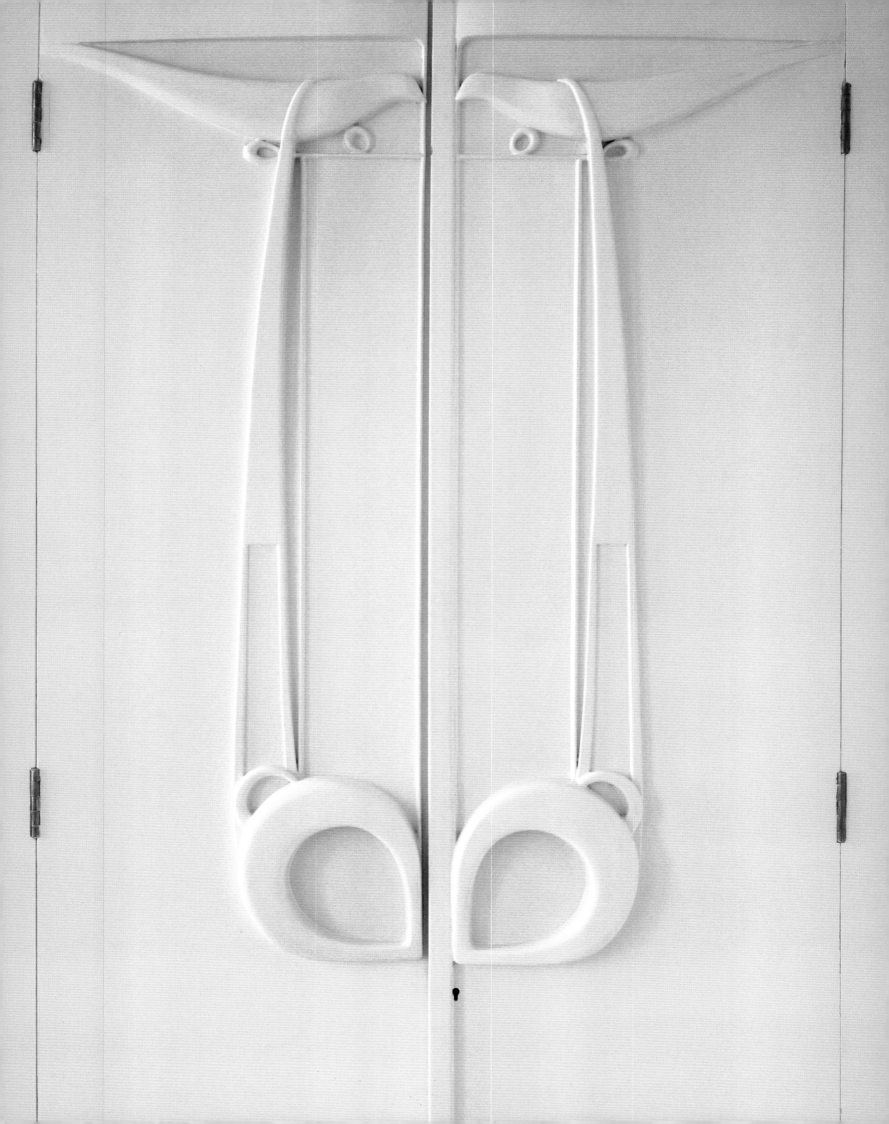

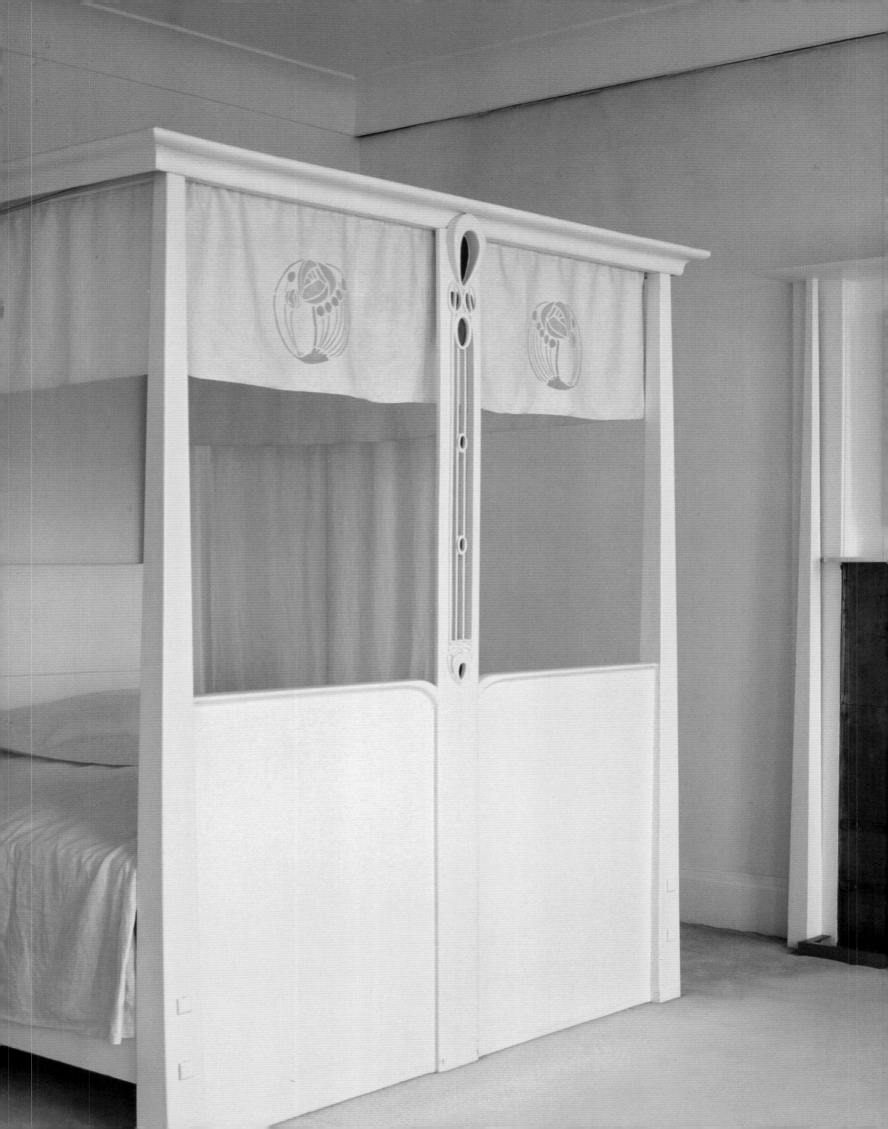

Blackie asked the young architect to build him a house that would be an exceptional work of art, and Mackintosh in turn asked his client to share his daily routines so that he could develop a clear understanding of the requirements. The result was a rustic villa, its facade covered with harling (a mixture of gravel and cement). The arrangement and varying sizes of the rooms determined the structure's final form. It was an "inside out" approach to architecture.

Even now, it is easy to imagine the astonishment of the first visitors to Hill House, a building that, according to Mackintosh, had no echo of a Palladian villa, English cottage, Swiss chalet, or Scottish castle. From the drawing room, with walls decorated with a stylized rose motif, to the bedroom furnished with organic forms, light and whiteness predominate. Creamy white, chalky white, eggshell white—white is present in all its nuances. Margaret MacDonald created decorative panels from stucco and stained glass, while her husband designed the ladder-back chair that was to become an icon of twentieth-century design. The bedroom was such a success that Mrs. Blackie made it her custom to receive guests there for afternoon tea.

The Mackintoshes' career success was short-lived, and in 1911, the couple, unable to get new commissions, moved to London. Art Nouveau was on the wane. Charles and Margaret packed their bags again and moved to Port-Vendres in the south of France where they tried to eke out a living selling watercolors. Charles Rennie Mackintosh died in London in 1928, suffering from cancer of the tongue, and Margaret died in 1933, also forgotten.

It was not until 1981 that Hill House regained its former splendor. Now visitors from every corner of the world can see that the work of Charles Rennie Mackintosh and his wife has lost none of its freshness. Their designs form a vital chapter in the great saga of architecture and design.

---

1. Thomas Howarth, *Charles Rennie Mackintosh and the Modern Movement* (London: Routledge Ltd., 1952), p. 31.

*

99: Detail of the carved and lacquered wood ornamentation on the doors of the armoire in Mrs. Blackie's bedroom. **100–101:** The drawing room in Hill House; with the exception of a painting by Margaret MacDonald above the fireplace, everything is by the architect himself. **102–3:** Nowadays, the high-backed "Ladder Chair" is reproduced by a major Italian firm. **104:** The hangings of the double canopy bed are decorated with fragments of colored glass and embroidered by Margaret MacDonald.

Hidden Treasures of Art Nouveau

Henry Van de Velde

The monuments of Art Nouveau have been meticulously documented down to the last detail, and among the giants of this important artistic movement, the Belgian Henry Van de Velde (1863–1957) stands out for his ability to combine architecture, interior decoration, and design in a *Gesamtkunstwerk* (total work of art) in which everything bears his distinctive signature: furniture, lighting fixtures, fabrics, stained glass, carpets, metalwork, books, silverware, vases, platters, silverware, garden furniture, and even the gowns and jewelry worn by the mistress of the house. Under Van de Velde's guiding hand, Art Nouveau became a leitmotiv, the thread that connected a new aesthetic with a modernism that presaged the now ubiquitous phenomenon of the "designer."

Influenced by the Arts and Crafts movement and the innovative designs of William Morris and Charles Voysey, Van de Velde turned his back on painting in 1892 to build his private residence, Villa Bloemenwerf, in a tranquil Brussels suburb. Photographic records of the period show a rustic house with a traditional facade, crowned with a three-gabled roof. However, the unconventional light-drenched interior is filled with elegantly simple furniture. Everything in the Van de Velde house is fresh, and everything is natural, fluid, devoid of artistic pretensions. This taste for asceticism and absence of ornamentation is evident in all of the architect's work, from his days as cofounder and director of the Kunstgewerbeschule (art school) in Weimar to the last plans he sketched on his design table during his forced exile in Switzerland. Skimming through the records documenting his long career, we come across important projects, including the Folkwang Museum in Hagen and the Kröller-Müller Museum in Otterlo, that

sometimes distract attention from the houses and villas that he designed for his private clients, including the Villa De Zeemeeuw in Scheveningen near The Hague and the Nietzsche Archive in Weimar.

"I've got a terrific amount of work to do before I can leave tomorrow for The Hague where I've been called to work on building a villa,"[1] wrote Van de Velde in July 1900 to his friend Eberhard von Bodenhausen, head of the pharmaceutical firm Tropon, for which the architect had designed posters. This villa, built for Doctor Leuring, would later be described by historians as the architect's last work in the Art Nouveau style. Its facade is marked by an arabesque—a Van de Velde signature—and an inscription with the words "Villa De Zeemeeuw" (Seagull Villa). Today the building still retains its exterior stairs, a sinuous construction of painted wood that descends from the loggia on the main floor to the garden. The lofty stairwell's far wall has a symbolist fresco executed by the Dutch painter and designer Johan Thorn-Prikker.

In contrast to the Villa De Zeemeeuw, the Nietzsche Archive in Weimar, located since 1896 in the Villa Silberblick, transformed and decorated by Van de Velde between 1902 and 1903 to house the archives of the philologist, philosopher, and poet Friedrich Nietzsche, has survived intact. It is generally supposed that one of Van de Velde's close friends, the collector and patron Harry Graf Kessler, persuaded Nietzsche's sister, the authoritarian Elisabeth Förster-Nietzche, to engage the architect.

With a budget of 43,000 deutsche marks at the time, Van de Velde had the resources to design a luxurious decorative scheme that culminated with the *Lesesaal* (reading room). The stove, benches, furniture, bookshelves, and white marble bust of Nietzsche by the sculptor Max Klinger form a perfectly unified whole. Viewing it today, we marvel at its flawless condition and wonder why such a masterpiece has not yet attracted the recognition it so richly deserves.

---

1. Henry Van de Velde, quoted in: Joop M. Joosten, "Henry Van de Velde en Nederland 1892–1902. Belgische Art Nouveau en Nederlandse Nieuwe Kunst" (Brussels: Cahiers Henry Van de Velde, numbers 12–13, 1974), pp. 6–46.

107: The door handles are typical of Van de Velde's austere aesthetic. **108–9:** Villa Leuring's stairwell, decorated by the symbolist painter Johan Thorn-Prikker and his assistant Jan Altorf using the *sgrafitto* technique (superimposing layers of plaster in various colors). **110:** Entrance door to the Villa Silberblick, with a decorative door handle of red and gold copper. **111:** Van de Velde designed an impressive copper stove for the library. The beech wood furnishings are the work of the cabinetmaker Scheidemantel. **112:** The white marble stele is by Max Klinger.

The Diva of Rue Jacob

Madeleine Castaing

Marie-Madeleine Magistry was born on December 19, 1894, in Chartres, to a large bourgeois family. Years later, she remembered every last detail of the over-decorated house where she grew up. She described the interior of the family residence as "a succession of dark rooms, decorated with an emphasis on blackened pear wood furniture and Louis XV and Louis XVI styles. It was enough to make you weep."[1] She was alluding to an era haunted by the lingering vestiges of the Victorian age, so strangled by a pathological prudery that it found even the legs of grand pianos to be unseemly, and covered them up with absurd little chintz skirts.

Swept away and married at the young age of fifteen to Marcellin Castaing (fourteen years her senior), who at the time was the mayor of Longages, a village in the Haute-Garonne, Madeleine had a brush with scandal. It was her first great experience in what was to be a long and extraordinary life, marked by a number of decisive turning points.

Detailed information on the privileged life of the glamorous Castaing couple is limited. There are a few photographs documenting Madeleine's first forays in the realm of decoration in their apartment in Nancy. Other snapshots show her looking pretty and stylish frequenting the cafes of Montparnasse, where she met Picasso and Olga Khoklova, attracting the notice of Braque, Léger, Brancusi, Chagall, and Modigliani, among others, befriending the painter Chaïm Soutine (she would later become his patron and muse), and winning over Erik Satie, a notorious misogynist, who often called upon her at her Paris apartment on rue Victorien-Sardou, as well as visiting her magnificent manor house in Lèves, near Chartres.

It was in fact in the magnificent Directoire style manor house set in a lovely park, a gift from her mother-in-law, that Madeleine Castaing's career as a designer truly began. Throughout her working life, she always defended the idea of a "living" house. She loathed sterile interiors that were an ostentatious effort to impress; instead, she vaunted the charms of houses filled with the happy clamor of children, cats, dogs, visiting friends, and lengthy fireside conversations. Lèves became both her family home and the site of her apprenticeship in interior design.

It was probably at Lèves that she first discovered the appeal of the Viennese Biedermeier style and English mahogany furniture. Perhaps it was then that she felt attracted to the amply padded comfort of a Napoleon III sofa bedecked with a fringe. She loved to bargain hunt among antiques dealers, the Saint-Ouen flea market, and neighborhood bric-a-brac stores, and anywhere else that offered a chance to come across something striking and unique. In her manor house in Lèves, Madeleine conceived and carried out a decorative scheme that embraced nineteenth-century opaline decorative articles, black and gold Regency furniture, Empire terra-cotta busts, flowery chintzes, lamps topped with turquoise blue and jade green paper shades, and cast iron swan-neck gondola beds.

Many years later, when Paris was engulfed by a war that would change the course of history, she decided to open an antiques shop, initially located in the rue du Cherche-Midi in a shed that had originally housed the Madame Sans-Gêne laundry. In 1947, she moved her boutique to the corner of rue Jacob and rue Bonaparte. She decided to paint the facade black, and the story goes that jealous colleagues spread the rumor that a funeral home was about to move into the premises. In any case, the fame of Madeleine Castaing as an interior designer only continued its ascent.

The diva of rue Jacob died in December 1992, but the style that bears her name and her incalculable contribution to the world of interior design lives on undimmed by the passage of time. She believed that her ghost would return after her death, and who would venture to contradict her?

---

1. Conversations with the author.

115: In the reception room of the manor house in Lèves, the terra-cotta bust of a gentleman presides over the fireplace. The painted metal wall fixtures are the creation of the mistress of the house. **116–17:** Artfully arranged on the famous ocelot rug—a typical Castaing touch—nineteenth-century ceramic stools, and seats and armchairs from a variety of sources become sculptures in their own right. **118:** The legendary Castaing blue is everywhere. **119:** A nineteenth-century painted canvas on the wall behind Madame's bath. **120–21:** Madeleine Castaing filled the park of Lèves with statues and garden furniture that was weather-beaten by the passage of time. **122:** An enigmatic sphinx reposes on the shores of the lake.

A Refined Gentleman

Billy Baldwin

The American decorator Billy Baldwin was a goldmine of inspired quotations, and many pages could be filled with his judicious remarks. For example: "The best decoration in the world is a roomful of books," "Comfort is perhaps the ultimate luxury," and "If you have marvelous taste and know exactly what you want, you don't need a decorator."

A man of small stature and outsized talent, William Williar Baldwin Jr. was born in Baltimore in 1903 and grew up in a house designed by the noted New York architect Charles A. Platt. When Baldwin was a young boy, his parents gave him permission to decorate his bedroom however he wished, furniture included. Baldwin was so bitten by the decorating bug that, following a brief and disastrous career in his father's insurance company, he added the word "decorator" to his calling card. In 1935, the prominent New York designer Ruby Ross Wood summoned him to abandon Baltimore and become her assistant at a salary of thirty-five dollars a week. Baldwin was feeling suffocated in his native town and later proclaimed that there were no more than three French chairs in the entire city; he packed his bags and boarded the next train.

In no time, New York was worshipping at his shrine, and society ladies were aflutter about this well brought up little fellow, impeccably attired and undeniably stylish. He saw himself as an unrivaled colorist first and foremost; he decorated the apartments of his clients in bright colors inspired by the paintings of Henri Matisse. One anecdote about Baldwin refers to a shade of green he selected for the living room of a house in Palm Beach: it claims that he held out a gardenia leaf to the painter, spat on it, and instructed him to copy the color, spit included.

Billy Baldwin bequeathed an invaluable legacy to the world of design, but regrettably his creations have come down to us only in the form of photographs published in a handful of books and in specialized shelter magazines. Thanks to these images, we know that this decorator so favored by society women, including Babe Paley, Rachel Mellon, Jacqueline Kennedy Onassis, and the formidable Diana Vreeland (for whom he designed a living room with walls covered in bright red, floral fabric because she had asked him for "a garden in hell"), loved cotton fabrics, walls lacquered in chocolate brown, lamp bases fashioned from plaster, rattan tables, and abundant use of straw and bamboo, real or fake. The library lined with slim brass columns that he designed for Cole Porter's apartment in New York's Waldorf Towers has come down to us as one of the twentieth-century's most iconic designs. Otherwise, intact Baldwin interiors are extremely rare.

Several years ago, the New York decorator Sam Blount received a commission to restore an interior previously decorated by Baldwin in a Greek Revival house in the Garden District of New Orleans. Blount arrived to find a neoclassical residence with the distinguished air of a Greek temple and numerous decorative details that revealed Baldwin's distinctive touch. Working in collaboration with the architect James Fox, Blount was able to retain the spirit of the great designer, his predilection for bright colors, and his love of comfort. Today, the house reflects the relaxed sense of style that prevails in great southern houses. While respecting the house's historic character and the famous Baldwin touch, Blount successfully introduced his own classic, elegant style.

Billy Baldwin retired from his sophisticated artistic life in 1973 to live on the New England island of Nantucket. A year earlier he had published the book entitled *Billy Baldwin Decorates*, the apotheosis of a style and taste that ended with his death in 1984.

✳

125: The convex star-shaped mirror above the fireplace reflects a distorted image of the living room. **126:** The stairwell with its decor of fluted columns, bell-shaped lighting fixture, and walls covered with panoramic wallpaper is typical of early nineteenth-century patrician homes. **127:** The Regency mirror is crowned with three feathers, the heraldic emblem of the Prince of Wales. **128–29:** The English-style furniture dating to the late eighteenth and early nineteenth centuries is an integral part of the American federal style. **130:** A Louis XVI armchair is upholstered in an ocelot print. The screen with its panoramic decoration dates from the first half of the nineteenth century. **131:** In the bedroom, the Louis-Philippe style beds are covered in green velvet. **132:** Sam Blount lacquered the walls in the library in bright red.

Italian-Style Elegance

Stefano Mantovani

Italians have a taste for design in its purest form and willingly leave the frescoed halls of their baroque palaces almost empty, content with a single sofa covered in white linen and a lighting fixture as tall and slim as an exclamation point. But there is also a Jekyll and Hyde aspect to this personality profile, a predilection for gilded consoles, marble columns and busts of Roman emperors, and crystal and Murano glass chandeliers. It takes all kinds to make a world, and in this particular world, the *éminence grise* of Italian designers, Stefano Mantovani, is preeminent.

In his youth, Mantovani pursued studies in architecture as convention dictated, but he failed to find his true vocation because his real passion was interior decoration. He took a lavish approach to decor that employed shimmering fabrics, paintings by the great masters, period furniture, and gleaming gilt work everywhere. At the beginning of his career, important clients, such as the renowned Valentino Garavani, commissioned him to create custom-designed exotic, opulent decors. With the passage of time, Mantovani's name became synonymous with a hyper-classical style that reflected first and foremost the social status of his clients. Apart from a few aberrations, including a collection of pop art furniture that he designed in the 1980s, the Mantovani style remained resolutely rooted in classicism. The highly successful facelift he gave to the long-established Ambasciatori Hotel in Rome, today known as the Ambasciatori Palace Hotel, is just one example.

As is so often the case with great designers, Mantovani's own apartment, tucked within a venerable palazzo around the corner from the Palazzo Borghese, is an exhaustive anthology of his decorative preferences.

His apartment is very spacious, its many large rooms pervaded by a pleasing chiaroscuro. The decorator and his partner and collaborator Manuel Jimenez invite us to linger and relish a *dolce far niente* experience. The ambiance is inarguably inspired by nineteenth-century romanticism. Paintings of exotic subjects and deep armchairs slip-covered in white cotton or upholstered in silk damask create a Proustian setting that would have appealed to film director Luchino Visconti. In the home of Mantovani and Jimenez, as in all the other interiors they have designed, the mood is relaxed and serene. An abundance of cushions lies heaped on the sofas; paintings, drawings, and engravings cover almost every inch of wall space; the muted lighting judiciously highlights a beautiful collection of *objets d'art* and keepsakes.

The decorator would not be worthy of his Roman heritage had he not decorated his bath in the taste of a *grand seigneur*. With large-scale paintings, a drawing signed by the classical painter Carlo Maria Mariani, an ancient marble fragment, and antique furniture worthy of an elegant reception room, the bathroom has become an additional living space. In Rome, all roads lead to the discreet luxury that bears Stefano Mantovani's distinctive signature.

*

135: Sumptuous fabric is used to cover a Louis XV loveseat in the smoking room. The cushions are slip-covered in blue and white ikat. 136–37: Large nineteenth-century paintings cover almost every inch of the smoking room walls. 138: A magnificent painting of the Italian school dominates the living room. The wall paneling has inlaid mirrors. On the Empire chest, the designer has arranged part of his collection of Chinese porcelain statuettes. The slip-covered armchairs are typical of his low-key, stylish approach. 139: The bathroom walls are covered with nineteenth-century paintings and drawings. 140: Another view of the bathroom. The drawing is by Carlo Maria Mariani.

The *Eminence Grise* of Marrakech

Bill Willis

The American designer Bill Willis arrived in Marrakech in 1966. He was traveling with Jean Paul Getty, Jr., and his wife Talitha Pol, who were on their honeymoon and planned to spend a few weeks in the Red City (*El Hamra* in Arabic).

Born in Memphis, Tennessee, Willis willingly confesses that he had a difficult youth. He always dreamed of a career in the arts and was admitted to the highly competitive Cooper Union for the Advancement of Science and Art in New York and later to the École des Beaux-Arts in Paris. However, he readily admits that he learned the "real" business of decorating from the formidable Roslyn Rosier, one of the most visible decorators in the pre war years, whose architectural office and antiques shop were located on 57th Street. Willis loved gossip and would regale audiences with how Miss Rosier doubled her prices when dealing with wealthy socialites like Mrs. Vanderbilt and Babe Paley. One day he walked out the door forever because he could no longer put up with his boss's intrigues. Shortly thereafter, in 1962, he crossed the Atlantic and set up shop on his own on the Via Gregoriana in Rome. There he made the acquaintance of the son of the super-rich American businessman Jean Paul Getty and his gorgeous Indonesian-Dutch wife Talitha.

During his first visit to Marrakech, Willis was dazzled by the gracefulness of the architecture, the beauty of the colors, and the quality of the work done by Moroccan artisans. These skilled craftsmen continued to embellish the traditional houses known as *riads* in the medina with *ghebs* (stucco friezes), *zelliges* (multicolored mosaics), and doors decorated with *zouaq* (geometric motifs carved in wood and highlighted with color).

The most fascinating technique of all was the art of *tadelakt*, which he discovered in the city's hammams. This coating, consisting of lime that is colored, waxed, and polished with black soap and pumice stone, is impermeable. Willis brought it out of the hammam and introduced it in the city's most sophisticated houses, applying it lavishly to the walls of the grand residences that he later decorated for the Gettys, Rothschilds, Agnellis, Pierre Bergé and Yves Saint Laurent, Alain Delon and Mireille Darc, and Bernard-Henri Lévy and Arielle Dombasle. In 1972, he indulged himself with the purchase of a former harem, complete with hammam, tucked away in a narrow alley in the impoverished neighborhood of Sidi Bel Abbes.

Bill Willis inarguably reinvented Moroccan style. In addition to his celebrated revival of tadelakt, he should also be recognized for adding fireplaces to his houses. Thanks to the hearths designed by Willis, his clients can warm themselves up in front of a good wood fire; winter nights in Morocco can be pitiless, and the traditional ceramic *brasero* can only do so much.

Bill Willis died in 2009 of a cerebral hemorrhage in a hospital in the city he loved so much. The contents of his house were put on display in a warehouse and sold to his admirers. We still have the interiors of the palaces, houses, hotels, and restaurants that he designed, as well as the remembrance of a fascinating man. He would frequently receive guests in his erstwhile hammam, recounting bits and pieces of his life story and the most recent snatches of worldly gossip while seated next to the fire in his favorite Indian chair. His gestures were broad, his eyes rimmed with kohl. A bottle of bourbon and a brass ice bucket in the form of a Moroccan house were always within easy reach. An unforgettable memory.

✳

143: Bronze andirons in the form of dragons. **144:** For Bernard-Henri Lévy and Arielle Dombasle, Willis created a new space in an outbuilding of the Zahia Palace; it has the atmosphere of a château, thanks to a massive classical fireplace and an eighteenth-century tapestry. **145:** In one of the palace's bathrooms, the decorator added a stucco fireplace decorated with a fish scale design. **146–47:** In Marrakech, Willis respected the authentic ornamentation executed by highly skilled artisans and designed multicolored mosaics, lacelike stucco motifs, and carved, painted cedar wood. **148:** Willis designed fireplaces that are directly inspired by traditional Moroccan designs.

The Ghosts of the Palazzo Merati

Emile Targhetta d'Audiffret de Gréoux

For many years at the official opening of the Venice carnival, a group of gorgeously disguised revelers followed the distinctive figure of a man across the Piazza San Marco; his elegant physique and richly embroidered garb evoked the charms of the legendary seducer Giacomo Casanova. Venetians, and all those who returned each year to celebrate Mardi Gras in the city known as the Serenissima, were familiar with this eccentric character. However, few were aware that he was none other than the Count Emile Targhetta d'Audiffret de Gréoux, who lived on the *piano nobile* of the Palazzo Merati.

Born to an old aristocratic family in San Remo in 1916, the count was always a colorful character. At an advanced age, he decided to settle in Venice. The Venetian aristocracy took a dim view of the count's arrival, regarding him as an interloper. They could hardly approve of a "foreigner" having the temerity to occupy the *piano nobile* of the ancient palazzo attributed to the architect Andrea Tirali, built in the early seventeenth century for Stefano Protasio, a wealthy Venetian merchant. His detractors were unaware that the count had long ago been bitten by the decorating bug, that he was a gifted painter in his spare time, and that he was cooking up a plan to redecorate the *piano nobile* by adding trompe l'oeil ornamentation, charming frescoes, and portraits by his own hand. The count did not shrink from scaling ladders to paint the ceiling of his modest foyer with baroque motifs. He embellished the reception room with faux marble and *sopraporta* of the highest quality.

The count had another passion: disguises. He was very clever with his hands and knew every detail of eighteenth-century garments by heart. Over several decades,

he amassed a costume collection of unequalled sumptuousness. He was delighted to have acquired the actual location where Casanova was arrested. He would proudly show his distinguished guests the alcove decorated with exuberant plaster carving by Abbondio Stazio and Carpoforo Mazzetti Tencalla where the great seducer took refuge before being incarcerated in the *piombi*, the prisons located just beneath the lead roof of the Doge's Palace. The count took an almost childish pleasure in playing the role of a period character in a period setting, but the undeniable elegance of that setting with its enormous, multicolored Murano glass chandeliers, marble busts, tapestries, and authentic furnishings, combined with meticulously contrived disguises, forestalled ridicule, transforming the count into a living piece of performance art.

Emile Targhetta d'Audiffret de Gréoux died in July 2008, and today the *piano nobile* of the Palazzo Merati seeks an interested buyer. Will the new owner inherit the ghosts of Giacomo Casanova and the eccentric count?

∗

151: A view of Count Targhetta's remarkable collection of costumes. **152:** Antique tapestries, marble busts, eighteenth-century Venetian furniture, and Oriental rugs. **153:** In the reception room of the *piano nobile*, an eighteenth-century Murano glass chandelier reflects the room's extravagant decor. The master of the house executed the painted decoration on the exposed beams. **154–55:** The faux-marble of the *sopraporta* was also the work of the count. **156:** The ceiling with its cartouches was designed by the count. **157:** Old master paintings and baroque decoration. **158:** In his bedroom, the count arranged a charming still life with a Louis XV wall clock and eighteenth-century family furniture. **159:** The count enjoyed pointing out how various details of the stucco decor (seen from the bed) were unabashedly erotic. **160:** In the antechamber, a portrait of the count's mother is propped against an antique drapery. The eighteenth-century console is Venetian.

An American in Spitalfields

Dennis Severs

The late Dennis Severs was an American anglophile who was fascinated by the English eighteenth century. As a very young man, he longed to leave his native California and embark on an exploration of London—particularly the London of the Georges, the city pictured in William Hogarth's inimitable illustrations for *A Rake's Progress*, every detail of which—every interior, every piece of furniture, every single objet—he knew by heart.

Arriving in London in 1967, Severs set out on a thorough exploration of the city on foot. He left much-visited historical monuments and attractions to the touristic hordes. Charting his own course, he was amazed to find miraculously well-preserved houses in the East End, a neighborhood once occupied by Huguenot silk weavers, Protestants exiled from their native France. Rundown and lacking virtually any modicum of modern comfort, they had miraculously retained their period details (shutters, ceilings, fireplaces, and stairways), as well as spacious workshops tucked beneath the eaves. Severs immediately purchased one of these houses located at 18 Folgate Street.

Today, the Severs house is a rare jewel in a neighborhood now besieged by the fevered pace of modernization. Beyond the entry door, visitors enter a time machine that carries them back far from our frenetic era.

During his lifetime, Severs never revealed exactly when he conceived of the Jarvis family, an imaginary dynasty of Huguenot silk workers who were the hypothetical residents of this house. He probably wanted to create a "lived in" atmosphere from the outset. In his own words: "With something for the eyes, something for the nose, and something for the ears."[1]

The period decor he created for the Jarvis family was far from a fantasized reconstruction. As visitors wander among upholstered wing chairs, family portraits, period tea services, canopy beds, and even (in the interest of authenticity) chamber pots, they have the impression of entering the family's private life unbidden.

When he first opened the house to curious visitors who proved eager to "take a tour of the eighteenth century," Severs demonstrated that they would gain a better understanding of Hogarth's era by exploring Folgate Street than by making the rounds of the châteaux and palaces of the same period. The ambiance of the house was permeated with memorabilia of days gone by: Madame Jarvis had forgotten her fan on a chair and left her makeup out on her dressing table. Thanks to an ingeniously concealed audio system, there were fragments of conversation in the entry hall, a door slamming in the distance, footfalls on the staircase, and the clatter of a horse-drawn carriage passing in the street outside.

Dennis Severs was not an interior designer in the strict sense of the term, but the house he has left us demonstrates his singular talent for decoration and all aspects of this fascinating endeavor, whether selecting an armchair, a color, a carpet, or just a simple porcelain bowl. The National Trust now preserves the artistic legacy bequeathed by Severs and continues his tradition of guided visits and candlelit nighttime excursions. Dennis Severs has indeed won his wager.

---

1. Conversation with the author.

＊

163: The paneling and shutters in the small parlor were painted dark green to approximate the atmospheric chiaroscuro that characterizes the genre paintings of Hogarth and his contemporaries. The deliberate disorder, carefully created from items dating from the period, evokes a trompe l'oeil panel. **164–65:** Garlands of gilded nuts and ribbons hanging around the mantelpiece suggest that Christmas is fast approaching. **166, 167:** A great aficionado of Dickens, Severs transformed the top floor to give it the atmosphere of a wretched, dilapidated hovel typically referred to as "Dickensian." **168:** Every detail in the bedroom has been scrupulously observed, from the eighteenth-century waistcoat hung on the door to the draperies on the period bed, illuminated by a candle.

In the Gustavian Style

Lars Sjöberg

Lars Sjöberg, the curator of the Nationalmuseum in Stockholm, a writer, collector of eighteenth-century furniture and manor houses, and acclaimed guru of the Gustavian style, destroys houses in order to save them. Sjöberg may well be the only proprietor in the world who scrapes down walls instead of replastering them, rips up entire rugs to expose the wooden parquet and floorboards beneath, and strips out electrical wires and piping to restore the "naked" aspect of his most recent acquisition, giving it back the authenticity that modern comforts have, in his view, destroyed.

Admiration for the Gustavian style is deep-seated and longstanding in the Sjöberg family. Lars's father Bengt was a highly accomplished woodworker who made copies of the furniture and mirrors created during the reign of King Gustav III. His mother Lillemor patiently scraped down authentic furniture that had been repainted in order to discover its original color. Ursula, Lars's wife and right hand, is an appraiser of Gustavian furniture for a renowned auction house and has collaborated on books on the eighteenth-century Swedish art of living.

It is hardly surprising that the Sjöbergs live in a period house surrounded by period furnishings, but the fact that they collect manors and castles as others might collect stamps is rather remarkable. Equally remarkable is their unconditional devotion to authenticity, whether it be the authenticity of a piece of furniture, a stove, an article of faience, a fabric, or a lighting fixture. They are willing to relinquish every modern comfort to live by candlelight, and sit on a magnificent *rokokosofa* that is ill adapted to the curve of their backs. They also have little interest in things they consider "useless,"

including central heating and toilets. What matters to Lars and Ursula is the beauty of a patina, the form of an armchair, the weave of an old fabric, the decorative effect of a bust or neoclassical medallion in stucco, and the unique ambiance that pervades their houses and allows them to live almost outside of time.

Lars's passion has inspired European and even intercontinental enthusiasm for the *Gustaviansk* style, which is noted for the simplicity of its forms and the freshness of its colors. It is of course named after King Gustav III, a connoisseur of the arts with a particular fondness for everything French. Furniture painted in delicate shades of gray, checked fabrics, canopy beds with a rustic look, *moraklocka* (clocks that originated in the town of Mora), wide floorboards scrubbed down with a mixture of water and fine sand to give them a satiny finish, portraits of ancestors held captive in their oval frames, delicate crystal chandeliers, simple copper candlesticks, pedestal tables, and faience stoves are now making their way into our interiors. The Northern Star casts its benign light on all those who, like Sjöberg, dream of a manor house set on the shores of a lake as smooth as glass, or a proud castle as impressive as any Greek temple. In these idylls, they can live the good life in rooms filled with pale sofas and chairs and warm their hands around the ample mass of the traditional Scandinavian *kakelugn* stove.

In their château in Ekensberg, their manor house in Regnaholm, their charming private house in Odenslunda, as well as their other properties, the Sjöbergs enthusiastically continue to scrape down paneling and furniture, stripping walls to uncover a scrap of fabric or a patch of wallpaper. Their quest is to breathe new life into an era for which they are tireless ambassadors. Gustav III lives on because the style that bears his name has more verve than ever.

171: In the living room of the manor house in Hörle Herrgard, Lars has covered the walls, as well as the *rokokosofa* and stool, with a glazed cotton fabric in fuchsia. **172:** On the main floor of the manor house in Ekensberg, the corridor is filled with Gustavian furniture. The tall longcase clock has Chinoiserie decoration. **173:** The entrance hall of the manor in Sjöbo has a collection of eighteenth-century furniture and objects belonging to Sjöberg. **174:** A room with stripped floorboards and bare walls provides a setting for a Gustavian armchair and table. **175:** A lovely eighteenth-century portrait hangs against a section of wall decorated with faux paneling Lars discovered under many layers of wallpaper. After careful stripping, the chairs revealed their original layer of paint. **176–77:** The bedroom of the Sjöbo manor house is entirely covered in printed cotton, a copy of period fabric that Lars found in another château. **178–79:** In the dining room of the manor house in Ekensberg, the table, chairs, and wall fixtures are copies of originals that were discovered and reproduced by Bengt Sjöberg. The portrait-medallion is a copy of an original work in plaster by Johan Tobias Sergel. **180:** Eighteenth-century family portraits, a wall covered with printed cotton, a blond wood table, and a simple copper candlestick eloquently express the essence of the *Gustaviansk* style.

The Renaissance of the Past

Jacques Garcia

Jacques Garcia is a true phenomenon; he delights, enchants, disturbs, intrigues, inspires, and alarms, but never leaves anyone indifferent. When you contemplate Garcia's work, you cannot remain unmoved. This incomparable designer, a veritable magician, has turned the decorating world upside down by transforming ruins into châteaux and châteaux into faux ruins.

Much has been written about Garcia, and countless photographs of his interiors have appeared in magazines and books. The Hôtel Mansart de Sagonne in Paris, the Château de Menou in the Nièvre, the many apartments decorated for an international clientele on several continents, and the decoration of famous Parisian hotels and restaurants, including Le Fouquet's, Ladurée Champs-Élysées, the Royal Monceau, L'Hôtel Hôtel (the former Hôtel du Bélier, where Oscar Wilde died), and the Hôtel Costes are unforgettably etched in our minds. His latest venue, the Hôtel La Mamounia in Marrakech, the favorite haunt of the great and the good of the world, is a true tour de force. But Garcia's uncontested masterpiece is his restoration of his castle in Normandy, the Château du Champ de Bataille, built in the seventeenth century for the Maréchal de Créqui and the former fief of the Harcourt family, which Garcia bought in 1992.

He comes from a family of modest means, but his childhood was enriched by parents who taught him about the beauties of historic French decorative styles and took him to visit châteaux. Jacques became a self-made man *par excellence*. He is a rare phenomenon in France, creating sumptuous interiors for high-powered clients, and his taste for luxury extends to the decor of his own residences.

Jacques Garcia would be the last to aspire to false modesty. In his decoration, he is high-handed and given to extravagant gestures. His decorative vocabulary includes splendid seventeenth-century tapestries, signed period sofas, and canopy beds crowned with plumes. Lushly padded armchairs are covered in velvet and silk damask, with an ocelot or panther skin tossed nonchalantly across a Napoleon III ottoman.

In contrast to what one might expect, the Garcia style has no hint of the feminine or frivolous. The imposing busts of Roman emperors set on marble pedestals, the sumptuous library filled with rare books and *objets d'art*, and the corridors lined with hunting trophies, butterfly collections, and preserved beetles lend a distinctly masculine ambiance to the Château du Champ de Bataille. Garcia has traveled extensively, and has so thoroughly steeped himself in the images of remarkable interiors in Russia, Sweden, and the palaces of Potsdam that his rooms are filled with faience stoves, bright colors, and chandeliers and decorative objects in the taste of the neoclassicist Schinkel and the Russian painter and architect Voronikhine.

In his decors, Jacques Garcia has the gift of being able to employ the faux to give the illusion of the genuine. His encyclopedic knowledge of styles allows him to evoke, down to the last detail, a salon from the era of Princess Mathilde Bonaparte (1820–1904), the smoking room of a Scandinavian baron, a boudoir that would have pleased Madame du Barry, and a dining room worthy of a head of state. Gazing through the windows of the château, the visitor is astonished to discover a park worthy of Versailles with a vast ornamental lake, fountains, cascades, a Roman temple, another shrine dedicated to Leda with walls encrusted with semiprecious stones, an aviary, greenhouses, an open air theater, broad alleys lined with manicured yew trees, and magnificently planted parterres. Truly the dwelling of a *grand seigneur*!

183: A spectacular view of the château and parterres from the lake with a fountain embellished with gilded dolphins. **184–85:** In the Salon d'Hercule, marble busts, basins, and columns inspired by antiquity (among which is the bust of a Roman emperor that belonged to Louis XIV) blend with seventeenth-century furniture. **186:** Two portraits of Marie-Antoinette on either side of the fireplace, one from the eighteenth century and the other neoclassical. **187:** A seventeenth-century white marble statue representing Chronos in the Salon d'Hercule. **188:** A day bed of gilt wood dating from the second half of the seventeenth century that probably belonged to the daughters of Louis XV; it was formerly in the reception room of the Hôtel Mansart in Sagonne. **189:** A magnificent seventeenth-century tapestry depicting the rape of Europa covered an entire wall of the reception room in the Hôtel Mansart. **190:** Inspired by neoclassical design, the designer created an entry hall worthy of a palace in his private apartment. The statue on the right represents Antinous, the handsome favorite of Roman Emperor Hadrian. **191:** Some details of the Empire style ornamentation on the doors of the apartment. **192:** With a cozy niche housing a faience heating stove and walls covered in subtle shades of blue, this little sitting room seems to be plucked right out of a Russian palace.

From Rags to Riches

Pierre-Hervé Walbaum

An evocative mélange of scents—dust, old paper, and stale tobacco smoke—drifts through the air. Outside, we hear the familiar neighborhood noises and the nearby clamor from the rue de Rivoli, but in these spacious rooms with their tobacco-brown walls, the atmosphere of an era long gone by endures. The French decorator Pierre-Hervé Walbaum well remembers his first visit years ago to his neighbors' apartment on the *bel-étage*, the building's high-ceilinged, most elegant floor. One does not readily forget a labyrinth of Empire era rooms left vacant and frozen in time.

Pierre-Hervé Walbaum's sterling reputation is based on his meticulous attention to authenticity and his encyclopedic knowledge of styles and periods. His penchant for eighteenth-century France, neoclassicism, and the Empire style has won him a sophisticated international clientele, who wish to match the quality of their period decors with that of the furniture and *objets d'art* they incorporate. Walbaum's decision to move into an apartment that had been neglected for decades, leaving its patina untouched, was surprising to say the least.

Walbaum is an inveterate collector who ceaselessly accumulates treasures that crowd his apartment, armoires, and attic to the bursting point. It is certainly no surprise that gilt bronze clocks, Directoire mahogany furniture, a statue of an Egyptian mummy in polychrome wood signed by the great cabinetmaker Georges Jacob, comfortably padded Napoleon III fireside chairs, classical busts, and an Empire period gondola bed shifted down one floor and moved into their new home as if they had never changed place.

It was an extraordinary move, initiated and orchestrated by Walbaum, and a unique adventure that no one would dare to emulate. Without his experienced eye, years of professional practice, and obvious talent, the move could easily have resulted in catastrophe: in this case the challenge was not to adapt the setting to the decoration, but rather to adapt the decorative scheme to the existing setting.

Built by Charles Percier and Pierre-François-Léonard Fontaine, an architectural duo who had the good fortune to be introduced to Napoleon by his future empress Josephine de Beauharnais, the building whose *bel-étage* is occupied by Walbaum reflects their predilection for an approach to classicism that was highly disciplined and elegant. Employing imposing facades, generously proportioned porte-cocheres, and spacious interior courtyards, the architects embraced a dignified style, and their apartments were in keeping with this approach. Pierre-Hervé Walbaum's residence has high ceilings, tall French doors opening onto a balcony with lovely ironwork, and most importantly an interior of an exemplary simplicity. The architectural embellishment is limited to just a few marble fireplaces and a broad stucco molding suggestive of paneling. This is the perfect setting for the decorator's collection of furniture and decorative objects, an ideal backdrop that is at once romantic and Balzacian.

Pierre-Hervé Walbaum not only has a knowledgeable eye when it comes to styles; he also has a gift for introducing a theatrical note to his decorative schemes. He is well aware of the effect created by a bust of Venus posed nonchalantly on a mantel or an Empire gondola bed positioned in the middle of the room. However, this demanding gentleman has no patience with facile effects and is just as demanding of himself as he is of his clients. He does not tolerate errors of taste, bad reproductions, or decorating blunders of any kind. Monsieur Walbaum is indeed a perfectionist—no other word will do.

∗

195: A magnificent carving of an Egyptian mummy in polychrome wood, signed by the great cabinetmaker Jacob, in the dining room. **196–97:** Against a backdrop of tobacco-brown walls, Walbaum has created a faux period decor, thoughtfully drawing on his collection of sofas, armchairs, paintings, and decorative objects dating from the nineteenth century. **198–99:** An artfully draped Etruscan red curtain and an Empire sleigh bed are all the decorator needs to create a typically Balzacian bedroom. **200:** The centerpiece of Sèvres bisque is from the eighteenth century.

"Haute Couture" Apartment

Gilles Dufour

As a boy, he dreamed of becoming a trapeze artist in a big circus, but life turned out to hold many surprises for Gilles Dufour. Today the impressive résumé of the man known as "the mercenary of fashion" recalls his birth in Lyon, his youth in the fashionable sixteenth arrondissement in Paris, his studies in the Lycée Janson-de-Sailly and the École des Arts Décoratifs, and his first meeting with Yves Saint Laurent and Pierre Bergé. They were intrigued by the quality of his fashion sketches but thought he was a bit too young to launch a career in haute couture.

Gilles Dufour has often commented that for him the real meaning of luxury is the power to create in complete freedom. This has been the mantra he has scrupulously applied during his time as a stylist with André Oliver and Pierre Cardin. It also defined his lifestyle during his frenetic and fruitful collaboration with Karl Lagerfeld at Chloé and Chanel, where he occupied a position of such importance that he was often referred to as the "prince consort."

Dufour is a man who knows what he wants, and he is very clear on what he loves most passionately: fashion, designing collections, his colleagues, his cordial relationship with the models, his personal icons (Brigitte Bardot and Mia Farrow), his close friends (Claudia Schiffer and Catherine Deneuve), creating clothes for the actresses in Chabrol's films, devoting himself to his work body and soul, and never shrinking from a potentially provocative gesture.

Gilles Dufour is never seen without his black-framed glasses, never wears anything but beautifully tailored classics, and could never conceivably be accused of poor taste;

as is the case for many artists with strong personalities, so-called "good taste" runs the risk of hobbling creativity. In his sixteenth-arrondissement apartment, he offers indisputable proof that you can turn up your nose at convention and be chic and bohemian at the same time, mixing styles and periods with no concern about what people might say.

Initially there was really nothing spectacular about Dufour's apartment. It certainly had well-proportioned spaces, but very little in the way of architectural detail. He started by choosing a very pale shade of yellow for his living room walls and scattered them with starfish painted coral red. Then he gave free rein to his imagination and his unbridled yen for accumulating furniture, objects, and paintings.

How best to describe the Gilles Dufour style of decorating? Perhaps he "dresses" his home as he would an elegant woman. That theory might explain the multicolored fabrics tossed with studied nonchalance over a side table, a generously proportioned sofa upholstered with garnet-colored velvet, another covered with his favorite fabric, a design by Madeleine Castaing, a sofa bed worthy of an Egyptian pasha, portraits, drawings, old master paintings, and feminine busts scattered throughout the many rooms of this deliberately chaotic dwelling that eloquently exemplifies the aesthetic appetites of the master of the house.

Dufour's apartment is the perfect reflection of a decorator who is unselfconscious, with talent to spare, keeping crazy hours; he is generous, provocative, a subtle colorist with a passion for culture, oscillating between the taste of a *grand seigneur* and the kitsch favored by floozies. Above all, he is an inventive mind that decorates conventional paper lampshades with shocking-pink wrapping paper and gives the place of honor to an object shaped like a caravel and made entirely from crystal beads. His celebrity nieces, the creative duo Victoire de Castellane and Mathilde Agostinelli, should be very proud of their famous uncle.

＊

203: In the living room, a side table is hidden beneath a printed wool skirt. **204–5:** A large, grandiloquent nineteenth-century painting by Eugène Deuilly depicting the suicide of Pyramus and Thisbe keeps company with a cardboard bust signed by Mathias [Robert] and Nathalie [Lété]. **206:** The library sofa is upholstered with a fabric designed by Madeleine Castaing. Coral-red starfish are scattered across the walls. **207:** Sketches, drawings, paintings, and busts are everywhere in Gilles Dufour's interior. The lampshade covered with preserved red rose petals is by Christian Tortu. **208:** Inspired by the cut-paper silhouettes of folk art, Dufour had himself represented in profile. The padded bed and the hat-shaped lampshade are his own designs.

The Art of Living with Contemporary Art

Frédéric Méchiche

It has now been almost fifty years since the French interior architect Frédéric Méchiche began devoting himself to decorating houses for an international clientele, offering them the very best of his talents. Those who know his work are aware of his love of art in all its forms, from tribal pieces to the decorative arts and contemporary creations. His very personal approach to combining these elements led to the development of the style that bears his name.

Frédéric was born in Algeria and came to Paris at a very young age. The image of white houses flooded with the intense sunlight of the Maghreb remained emblazoned in his memory. With his passion for design, it was an obvious step to enroll in the private design school École Camondo; from then on his life took a decisive turn.

It can be difficult to determine the exact moment when a great designer is born. Méchiche's first project was on such a vast scale that it catapulted him to the forefront of his profession. The embryonic form of the Méchiche style, with its startling combination of disparate styles and objects—a Regency chest, a Roman torso, and an African mask—had taken shape. It simply remained to develop it further by creating interiors that were distinguished by their tremendous cultural diversity.

Lofts filled with light, white walls covered with works of contemporary art, daring juxtapositions of a Directoire armchair and a compression sculpture by César, eighteenth-century *boiseries* used as a backdrop for a Louis XVI sofa covered in black and white stripes—these were the necessary steps in Frédéric's career that led to his becoming

known simply as Méchiche. For a while, at least. Like any artist wishing to discover new visual sensations, the decorator dreamed of fresh challenges.

Frédéric Méchiche has always held that art is priceless, and as one decorative commission has followed another, he has successfully demonstrated the truth of his words by giving a prominent place to everything he considers to be artistic expression: a gouache signed by Miró, a virtuosic watercolor by Christian Bérard, a photograph by Robert Mapplethorpe, an ink drawing from the hand of Karel Appel, as well as major works by Fabrice Hyber and Damien Hirst. All are welcome, as long as they fit seamlessly into interiors that bear his distinctive signature and harmonize perfectly with an authentic eighteenth-century chest, a vintage chair, or a Knoll coffee table.

The Méchiche look is not just a facile formula or "cocktail" of various periods, or an exercise in "mix and match" to obtain a novel result. It takes the hand of a master to juxtapose a piece of traditional furniture successfully with a contemporary work of art. Skimming through an album of Méchiche's most successful designs, the eye lingers over the unforgettable image of Hirst's *Spot Painting* hung over a neoclassical marble fireplace.

A designer of furnishings and decorative objects that are both classical and original, responsible for putting his signature stripes on everything from our furniture to our walls, Frédéric Méchiche can also lay claim to having created remarkable period decors by transforming sterile offices in an eighteenth-century *hôtel particulier*, creating and recreating period decors in period châteaux, and fitting out blandly decorated hotels with traditional, as well as resolutely contemporary, touches. In sum, Frédéric Méchiche has dressed the interiors of his time while casting a backward glance toward the past, and a forward look to the future.

211: A striking contrast between a neoclassical fireplace and Damien Hirst's *Spot Painting*. **212–13:** Méchiche transformed featureless offices in a Parisian building into an imposing reception room worthy of a grand *hôtel particulier*. The decor was entirely executed in staff plaster, and the decorator also designed an impressive sofa in the Georgian style. **214:** In an eighteenth-century château, a statue by Alberto Giacometti stands at the foot of a stone staircase. The ironwork is of the period. **215:** The rigorously Directoire style of Méchiche's private bathroom forms a startling contrast to a Victor Vasarely work hung above the metal tub and Harry Bertoia's No. 420C chair. **216:** When decorating a bedroom in an eighteenth-century château, Méchiche was inspired by Louis XVI decor and installed gray Versailles-style *boiseries* and a magnificent bed sumptuously draped *à la polonaise*. **217:** The walls of a small sitting room have been painted in trompe l'oeil to imitate grisaille wallpaper dating from the early nineteenth century. The console and the lidded jar date from the reign of Louis XV. **218:** The decor of this bathroom takes its inspiration from the neo-Gothic style, but avoids becoming a mere pastiche with its mint green walls and black and white tiles. **219:** In this bedroom, the far wall is covered in wide stripes. The patinated metal chaise longue is part of a collection of garden furniture that the decorator designed for a major manufacturer. **220:** A Comoglio fabric covers the walls and the *lit à la polonaise* in this bedroom of a château in Normandy.

A *Grande Dame* of Design

Andrée Putman

When Andrée Christine Aynard, who was born in 1925, received first prize for harmony from the prestigious performing arts school, the Conservatoire Nationale in Paris, from the hands of composer Francis Poulenc, he told her, without sugarcoating the news, that she did not have it in her to become a great composer. It was a difficult beginning for a young girl who had thus far led a sheltered life, dividing her time between her father's apartment on the rue des Grands-Augustins and the venerable Fontenay Abbey. It would have been difficult to foresee that she would one day become one of the world's foremost names in decoration and design.

Looking back on the early years of this woman who was to become an iconic figure, Andrée Putman faced a succession of unexpected obstacles and mishaps that eventually reached a happy ending. "The struggle against opposition creates invention,"[1] said Jean Cocteau, an expert on the matter. The young girl from a good family, who might have been destined for a bourgeois, unimaginative existence, became successively a messenger for the review *Femina*, and then worked for the magazine *Elle* and the art review *L'Œil*. After her marriage to the Belgian collector, editor, and art critic Jacques Putman, she surfaced as a stylist at Prisunic where she introduced a novel idea that attracted considerable press: selling lithographs by contemporary artists for the modest sum of 100 francs. In the late sixties, she had ties with the design studio of Denise Fayolle and Maïme Arnodin, known as MAFIA, and in 1971, she established Créateurs et Industriels with Didier Grumbach, a firm for the development of prêt-à-porter fashion and textiles.

Encouraged by her friend Michel Guy, Secretary of State for Culture during the presidency of Valéry Giscard d'Estaing, she established the agency Écart and began her ascension to international recognition in the realm of design. Fascinated by the work of designers who had receded into near oblivion, including Jean-Michel Frank, Robert Mallet-Stevens, René Herbst, and Eileen Gray, she opened the eyes of a new generation, reproducing their furniture, decorative objects, and lighting fixtures. From this point, it was just one more step to reach her ultimate goal: designing spaces and furnishing interiors.

In the 1980s, with her first installations in Morgans Hotel on Madison Avenue in New York in 1984, the commissions came flooding in. Putman then took on the architectural plans for Hotel Le Lac in Nagahama (Japan), the Hotel Im Wasserturm in Cologne (Germany), and the Sheraton at Paris's Roissy-Charles de Gaulle airport. These were quickly followed by the Carita hairstyling salon, the new Balenciaga and Azzedine Alaïa boutiques, Michel Guy's apartment, the office of the French Cultural Minister Jack Lang, and the Musée d'Art Contemporain in Bordeaux.

Described by Bernard-Henri Lévy as "an artist who is free in both her style and movements,"[2] Andrée Putman—who passed away in January 2013 at the age of eighty-seven—successfully shaped that freedom, restraining herself throughout her career from what can be the most pernicious freedom in the realm of decoration and design: excess. In the champagne bucket for Veuve-Clicquot, Guerlain's space on the Champs-Élysées, and the magnificent villa belonging to Bernard-Henri Lévy and Arielle Dombasle on the cliffs of Tangier, the *grande dame* of design always imposed limits on herself. Assisted in recent years by her daughter Olivia, she continued to win commissions and accolades, demonstrating that we should never forget just how far a person can go.

---

1. Jean Cocteau, quoted in: Barbara Stoeltie, *Rooms to Remember* (London: Frances Lincoln, 1998), p. 13.
2. Bernard-Henri Lévy, quoted in: Stéphane Gerschel, *Le Style Putman* (Paris: Assouline, 2005), p. 52.

223: In 1989, Andrée Putman decorated the new Balenciaga salon with trunks covered in chocolate-colored leather, trimmed with nails and lavish passementerie. **224:** In the Carita sisters' Paris salon, Putman covered the walls of the shampooing area with mosaics and designed a double sink in stainless steel. **225:** A marble sink and frosted glass wall inlaid with a mirror in the Carita ladies room. **226–27:** In Michel Guy's apartment, Putman developed a decorative scheme in neutrals to highlight the works of Lucio Fontana and Bram Van Velde. The armchairs are Louis XVI. **228:** The attic bedroom has a mood of cultural diversity. **229:** In the entrance hall, a large nineteenth-century painting forms a surprising contrast with a pair of Empire period chairs covered with horsehair and the Centimètre carpet designed by Eileen Gray. **230:** The erotically suggestive form of *Priape*, a bronze sculpture by Man Ray originally designed in 1920 and issued in a new white marble edition in 1968, inspired Putman in her design of the bathtub feet. **231:** In the stairwell of the villa in Tangier belonging to Bernard-Henri Lévy and Arielle Dombasle, Putman installed a reissued version of a floor lamp created in 1907 by Mariano Fortuny. **232, 233:** Austere and spare, with a rhythmic play of space and levels, the villa boasts timeless architecture and decor. **234:** Putman also designed the sofas with rounded armrests.

A Subtle Palette

John Saladino

Pale Amethyst, Periwinkle Blue, Light Taupe—no other designer so successfully describes and relishes the delicacy of the colors in his personal palette with the precision and sensuality of the *éminence grise* of American designers, John Saladino.

Born in Kansas City, Saladino studied at the University of Notre-Dame and the Yale School of Art and Architecture. However, it was not until he discovered Italy and Andrea Palladio, and became the personal assistant of the architect Piero Sartogo in Rome, that he found himself becoming one of the most visible exponents of classic interior design.

We of course recognize Saladino's admirable sense of proportion, his highly personal way of placing an object or piece of furniture, his uncompromising demands when considering the lighting of an object or a painting, but that does not tell the full story. As exercised by Saladino, the art of decoration is a visceral exercise, and this instinct is the basis for his choice of a color, fabric, antique tapestry, or even a bath towel.

"Perfection is too slick" is his oft-quoted maxim,[1] because the degree of perfection in Saladino's interiors risks the accusation of being too sterile to accommodate a fresco in the classical Roman style, an eighteenth-century armchair with the patina of age, a Directoire screen covered with old landscape wallpaper, or a time-ravaged neoclassical urn. John Saladino's interiors owe their perfection to imperfections in the details, such as the silhouette of an urn cut into a rusted iron plate from a ship's hull that looms over the mantelpiece of a New York dining room.

Examples of Saladino's distinctive decorative vocabulary abound. Consider the pastel palette that includes "Powder Beige," "Duck Egg Blue," and "Oyster White," that he deployed in an impressive Long Island residence to heighten the impact of a magnificent collection of paintings from the Romantic School. The Gobelins tapestries and antique rugs, Pompeian frescoes, and neoclassical landscapes known as *veduti* that he used to embellish an apartment near Park Avenue also deserve attention. And his restoration of a nineteenth-century clapboard house in central Massachusetts with its cinnamon-hued patinated walls and his exquisite selection of period furnishings must also be mentioned; here Saladino has proved his mastery of a historic restoration project.

A wooden house overlooking the Atlantic coast, an impressive "Tuscan" villa in California, a carriage house transformed into a residence in the middle of Manhattan, a penthouse with a view over Central Park, and a former ballroom transformed into a luxurious duplex apartment with a view of the New York skyline, all bear Saladino's signature. A unique signature that has left its mark on an era and will inspire generations to come.

----

1. John Saladino, quoted in: *Wilmington Morning Star*, March 27, 1990, p. 6.

*

237: The soft pink of the upholstery on the chaise longue and the pearl-white silk damask on the Georgian-style wing armchair are typical of Saladino's subtle palette. **238:** An Empire era portrait and an important work signed by William Bougereau dominate the light-filled living room. **239:** The dining room is furnished with a pair of tables to avoid excessive formality. **240–41:** The restoration of this nineteenth-century house in central Massachusetts was a real challenge for Saladino because his clients asked that he leave the patina of age and authentic features untouched. **242–43:** In the dining room of an apartment overlooking Central Park, the decorator created a classical decorative scheme, with his signature slip-covered chairs and an eighteenth-century English table. He cut the shape of a Medici vase into a rusty plate scavenged from the hull of an old ship. **244–45:** A very spacious Park Avenue apartment transformed into a *palazzo*: Pompeian frescoes, old master paintings of architectural vistas, and classic sofas upholstered with luxurious fabrics. **246:** In one corner of the dining room, a staff plaster urn stands on a fluted column.

A Photographer's Eye

François Halard

It is no secret that almost all successful interiors owe virtually all their appeal to careful composition. A photographic approach that gives the impression that the decorator sighted the room through a camera lens to find the most harmonious and advantageous position for each piece of furniture, each painting, and each decorative object. Houses owned and decorated by photographers are visible proof of this maxim. You could not find a more striking example of the principle than the *hôtel particulier* of the celebrated French interior and architectural photographer François Halard, located in one of the most historic sections of Arles.

François Halard began photographing interiors at the age of eighteen. It was a brilliant debut that instantly placed him among the ranks of the most promising talents of his generation. Son of the decorators and designers Michelle and Yves Halard, François grew up in beautiful houses decorated by his parents' masterly touch. They were welcoming homes and châteaux where the furnishings and objects had all been selected for their character. It should come as no surprise that François Halard was influenced by the hushed, romantic atmosphere that pervaded his childhood and dreamed of someday living in a house that would recall his earliest aesthetic experiences.

Frequently traveling all over the world for his many commissions, Halard chose Paris and New York as his home bases. However, when he came across an eighteenth-century *hôtel particulier* in Arles, he bought it without a second thought or asking many questions about its restoration: for him, the building's beauty was defined by its patina of age, walls covered by flaking paint, warped floors laid with hexagonal tiles,

parquet boards, and the limited availability of modern comforts. In hands other than those of a photographic artist, all those authentic touches would have disappeared forever, because so many people recoil when faced with beauty that is derived from dilapidation and the venerable patina of age.

Restoring an old structure while maintaining its original state requires extensive experience in the field, the patience of a saint, and tenacity in the face of every challenge. As a skilled photographer, François Halard possessed all these virtues and decorated his new home as if he was intimately familiar with it, reconstructing its decor from treasured personal memories.

Provence is hospitable to bright, glinting colors, but people seek shelter from the ferocity of the sun when they go inside. In François Halard's *hôtel particulier*, the rooms are bathed in a diffused light that flatters the period furniture he has accumulated since the early days of his youth, recent discoveries found in antiques shops and second-hand shops, souvenirs from his travels, and presents from his artist friends. Everything is arranged with the camera lens in mind and a deliberately bohemian air, demonstrating a unique ability to create an impression of being lived-in and spontaneous. François Halard is not a decorator in the strict sense of the term; he has visually absorbed the houses of his childhood, and with these treasures stored away in the portmanteau of his memory, he transformed his Arlesian home into a heartfelt homage to the artistic legacy of his parents.

*

249: The *hôtel particulier* sports a facade in typical Provençal colors. 250: François Halard left untouched the timeworn patina of his *hôtel particulier*, as can be seen in the staircase. 251: Wallpaper and frescoes from the eighteenth century and the Empire period cover the walls. The *à crosse* sofa with scrolled armrests is Louis XV, and the ceramic vases are contemporary designs. 252–53: A few examples of his singular ability to create a decor using a minimum of furniture and objects: a cast iron jardinière, a "witch ball," and a Louis XV sofa covered in red velvet. 254–55: The Louis XVI bed was among the fortunate finds of his youth. 256: The artist is fascinated by the beauty of flaking paint or a water-stained fresco.

An Illusionist Designer
Didier Rabes

Does a designer have a right to indulge in trickery when decorating a house? To fool the eye by creating Corinthian columns from paper-mache, Louis XV *boiseries* from painted stucco, Empire ornamentation from synthetic resins, and false doors with palatial pretensions that open onto blank walls? Ask that question of Didier Rabes, and he will answer in the affirmative, since Rabes is a devotee of decor that defies rules and conventions, whose inventiveness pays homage to the subtle art of illusion.

Rabes made his debut in the realm of decoration with the Parisian antique dealer and set designer Fersen, but he soon realized that the creation of an endless series of traditional decorative projects straight from the pages of *Plaisir de France* was not his cup of tea. Didier Rabes became an antique dealer himself and added the notation "decorator" to his business card.

One of Didier Rabes's first major projects was the conversion of the former couture workshop of Madeleine Vionnet in Paris. He achieved a veritable tour de force, brilliantly succeeding in marrying the authentic and the faux. He dived into his magician's hat and produced a decorative scheme evoking an eighteenth-century château, with an entrance hall in painted stucco that imitated the trophies on the *boiseries* of the Café Militaire. He continued with the transformation of the *piano nobile* in the Château d'Hérivaux near Chantilly, where he designed an entrance reminiscent of a hunting lodge, decorated with animal trophies and livery straight out of a theatrical production, a gallery decorated with *boiseries* that were actually a set of faux bois painted stucco walls, a dining room with recently produced "eighteenth-century Chinoiserie," and a park scattered with

neoclassical busts and thermae made of whitewashed plaster with a finish that makes them appear to be Cararra marble.

Leave the purists to denounce these acts of deception. Consider instead Didier Rabes's theatrical approach that relishes turning up its nose at authenticity and has no shame when it comes to juggling appearance and reality. Consider his conversion of four maid's rooms under the eaves of a *hôtel particulier* where he has installed his office, transforming the space into a Russian dacha. This is really the height of audacity and inventiveness, and the result of an ironic intellectual approach that the English entertainingly call "tongue-in-cheek."

The most recent book penned by a writer or last picture painted by an artist is always the best. Such is the case for Rabes's latest foray into decoration, a *hôtel particulier* in northern France that he keeps for his family and friends. The visitor will not be surprised: as you will have guessed, the monumental entry gate in the Louis XV style is a mere youth, the potted laurel trees in the courtyard are artificial, and even the *jardin à la française* never needs watering. Everything or almost everything in the home of Didier and Annick Rabes is illusion: the ocher marble niches on the landing, the brick walls in the kitchen, the Meissen porcelain in the living room—even the Louis XV armchairs and the Napoleon III fireplace chairs are products of our own century.

Every decorator has an undisputed masterpiece, and the real tour de force for Didier Rabes is the dining room. A dining room worthy of a Scandinavian manor house or a Baltic castle, a veritable apotheosis of blue and white, as exquisite as a porcelain box and decorated with Louis XV furnishings painted white, a rococo faience chandelier by Capodimonte, and baroque *torchères* of immaculate white surmounted by Chinese vases. Needless to say, it is all just an illusion and no one should trust appearances here. This is Didier Rabes's home, after all. And when we visit the home of Didier Rabes, we feast on beauty and illusion without asking too many questions.

259: In the dining room, the gilt and polychrome console is a resin copy of an eighteenth-century original, and the portrait of a distinguished lady, on the lower right, was touched up to lend an air of exoticism. **260–61:** In the entrance to a *hôtel particulier*, Rabes designed staff plaster ornamentation inspired by the *boiseries* of the former Café Militaire that were created by Claude-Nicolas Ledoux. The marble statues are from the eighteenth century. **262:** The furniture, chandelier, and paintings are authentic; the rest of the decor is attributable to Rabes alone. **263:** In this eighteenth-century château, Rabes created a large gallery with period furniture, a copy of an Empire period carpet produced in China, and plaster "*boiseries*" that imitate oak paneling. **264–65:** The château's nasturtium-yellow bedroom is furnished in the Chinese Chippendale style with trellises in the form of a pagoda and walls decorated with a tree of life design. **266–67:** Wooden trellises covered with vines (all of plaster), a hanging light fixture shaped like a basket, and a ceiling painted in trompe l'oeil transform this bathroom. **268–69:** Rabes converted a traditional apartment from the beginning of the last century into an eighteenth-century *hôtel particulier*. Surprise: everything from the Coromandel lacquer screen to the Russian chairs, Chinese vases, and Regency mirror is actually authentic! **270–71:** In the dining room of Rabes's own house, the Capodimonte faience chandelier, caned Louis XV chairs, Chinese vases, and rococo wall consoles are copies, and the walls decorated like German cabinets made of porcelain were executed by gluing on passementerie trim and household linens. **272:** Faux marble, faux coral, and faux Empire vase: the illusion is complete.

An Extraordinary Set Designer

Cesare Rovatti

Cesare Rovatti, the doyen of Italian decorators, can boast of being among his country's greatest set designers, as well as a costumer and decorator. His many collaborations with the giants of film, sometimes referred to as "the seventh art," including Luchino Visconti, Vittorio De Sica, Michelangelo Antonioni, Pier Paolo Pasolini, and Mauro Bolognini, have earned him international renown.

Born in Mortara, near Pavia, this eternally youthful gentleman, now in his eighties, delights in recounting his studies at the Brera Academy in Milan and his numerous collaborations with legendary colleagues including Pier Luigi Pizzi and Piero Tosi; he worked as their assistant for *Death in Venice* and *The Leopard*. Although his name is listed in the credits for the films *Romolo e Remo* (*Duel of the Titans*), *Ieri, oggi, domani* (*Yesterday, Today and Tomorrow*), and *Un bellissimo novembre*, Rovatti was evidently not unduly impressed by his achievements in the field: in the early 1970s he left the Cinecittà studios and their artificial world to create real decors for actual houses.

Cesare Rovatti's designs are often described as classics because they are filled with allusions to a distant past; however, this description is less than complete and does not accurately express the scope of his work. While Rovatti mines his impressive cultural repertoire and proclaims unbounded admiration for ancient Rome, the Renaissance, and the Italian eighteenth century, he also casts an admiring glance at the Stile Liberty (the fashion in Italy around 1900), the neo-Gothic, Art Deco, and contemporary design.

One of a long line of Italian designers including Renzo Mongiardino, Toni Facella Sensi, Maurizio Chiari, and Federico Forquet, Rovatti loves to design luxurious interiors

where the eye lingers pleasurably on chairs upholstered in velvet and silk, master paintings and drawings, antiques, sculptures, and decorative objects of the finest quality. In his own home in Rome, located in the former atelier of the painter Adolfo de Carolis, which occupies the upper floors of a building constructed in the style of a Roman villa, the tone is neoclassical. However, when Carla Fendi, one of the sisters of the legendary Fendi dynasty, commissioned him to convert and decorate her 1960s era villa at the foot of Monte Circeo midway between Rome and Naples, he designed a resolutely contemporary ensemble.

Built on the seacoast around 1960 by the architect Lucio Costa, Villa Ina is one of the jewels of Sabaudia, a town built in 1933 in 235 days by 600 workers on the orders of Mussolini. Its metaphysical architecture seems to be straight out of the paintings of Giorgio de Chirico. With the assistance of Simona Formilli-Fabrizzi and Fabrizio Talienti for the decoration, and the landscape architects Antonella and Francesco Fornai for the gardens, Rovatti conjured up a luminous and astonishingly fresh ensemble built around Costa's original construction—a white tower—with a spiral staircase, creating an immaculately white interior where contemporary design and art hold a preeminent place.

Cesare Rovatti has always emphasized that he draws inspiration from the personality of his clients and listens intently for the inner voice of the houses he decorates. This is the theme that runs through his career, allowing him to pass almost imperceptibly from the illusion of the blank white movie screen to the reality of interior decoration.

*

275: Villa Ina, once a simple white tower, was transformed by Rovatti with the addition of outbuildings and a spiral staircase that soars up to the terrace. **276–77:** In the living room, the white walls are a striking contrast to the armchairs covered with orange and sky blue leather produced by Arflex. The andirons are by Gio Ponti. **278:** The large circular sofa, covered with white leather, that occupies the entire lower part of the living room, is of Rovatti's own design. **279:** A work by Lucio Perone covers one of the dining room's walls. The table was designed by Piet Hein and Bruno Mathsson, and the chairs are by Arne Jacobsen. **280–81:** The circular bed was designed by Ron Arad. The coverlet is a patchwork of faux fur, and the artwork on the bedroom wall is by Lucio Perone. **282:** Cesare Rovatti created a fully transparent kitchen.

The Antiquarian of the Future

Yves Gastou

The antique dealer Yves Gastou is a pioneer, and it suffices to follow the development of his career and his taste in the field of design and decoration to realize that he has truly earned his sobriquet, "the antiquarian of the future."

Born in Carcassonne in 1948, Yves Gastou began his career in antiques with an internship with a dealer in his native city who specialized in eighteenth-century furniture. But he was already directing an appraising eye at more recent periods, and in 1970, he opened his own boutique where he sold Art Nouveau furniture and objects. In 1975, he could be found in a shop in Toulouse, where he mounted a defense on behalf of Art Deco, and in 1981, he had a stand in the flea market in Saint-Ouen, where he displayed Italian glassware by Flavio Poli, among other offerings. The next step in his ascent occurred in 1985, at 12 rue Bonaparte, where he created a sensation among the Parisian smart set with a retrospective of the work of Ettore Sottsass, a figure at the forefront of the Memphis Group of designers. Sottsass also created the gallery's interior design and its extraordinary multicolor terrazzo facade. Gastou then moved to the gardens of the Palais-Royal, to an exhibition space he dedicated to 1940s and 1950s styles, as well as modern design. In 1996, he first exhibited at the Paris Biennale des Antiquaires—the ultimate recognition for Gastou—where he introduced the styles of the 1940s at a show that formerly would have closed its doors to any artistic creation made after 1930.

Yves Gastou has a voracious eye, endless curiosity, and a horror of barriers. He is always on the lookout for something new, searching for what lies beyond current trends.

Along with his passion for decoration, the antique dealer also has a gift for adorning his clients' houses with exceptional pieces acquired through his gallery.

The word may seem exaggerated and even a bit passé, but one adjective suffices to describe Gastou's interiors: chic. Chic and elegant, because the man who helped us rediscover exceptional designers such as André Arbus, Jacques Quinet, Marc du Plantier, Gilbert Poillerat, and Jean-Charles Moreux will tolerate only interiors that combine originality and elegance.

Yves Gastou is fearless when it comes to mingling styles and periods. He does not flinch from using eighteenth-century oak paneling as a backdrop for a cast iron chair by Poillerat, an enormous stucco Art Deco bas-relief hung strategically at the top of a staircase leading to a mezzanine, or a Murano glass chandelier signed by Gio Ponti in a dining room paneled in absinthe green. Anyone who thinks that he will stop there and continue to elaborate on a theme with proven success is mistaken, because this energetic man on rue Bonaparte is already in hot pursuit of the newest discoveries. In 2012, Gastou cast his discerning eye on pop art furniture and Japanese manga and—for the moment at least—Mickey Mouse armoires produced by Disney have displaced chests by Arbus. But just for the moment, because with Yves Gastou you never know what tomorrow will bring.

*

285: The stucco bas-relief at the top of the staircase leading to the mezzanine dates from the 1930s and shows a scene from Kipling's *Jungle Book*. **286–87:** In the living room, everything seems to revolve around the Renaissance-style fireplace that is crowned with a bas-relief and a pair of girandoles. The Aubusson tapestry is signed by Jacques Despierre, and the furniture and decorative objects date from the first half of the twentieth century. In the office area, there are klismos chairs by T. H. Robsjohn-Gibbings. **288–89:** In an eighteenth-century *hôtel particulier*, the period *boiseries* harmonize beautifully with the furniture and tapestry that bear the signatures of André Arbus and Gilbert Poillerat. **290:** A large painting by Marc du Plantier dominates Yves Gastou's former dining room. The table's centerpiece is of porcelain bisque from the Sèvres manufactory. **291:** In the dining room of a Parisian *hôtel particulier*, a Murano glass chandelier complements the Louis XVI *boiseries* perfectly. **292:** The delicate profile of a bronze chair by Gilbert Poillerat stands out against the light wood eighteenth-century *boiseries* with fluted pilasters.

A Talent from the North

Anne Paul Brinkman

When he was scarcely seventeen years old, the Dutch designer Anne Paul Brinkman opened an antique and collectibles shop in his native town of Groningue, in the northeastern Netherlands. On his opening announcement, he glued a photograph showing him standing in front of his store: very handsome, very tall, and very slim, with long hair down to his shoulders, dressed in a checked shirt and overalls, with wooden shoes on his feet. Beside the photograph, he wrote: "Won't you come and have a look?" Enchanted by the young man's charm and candor, people thronged to the store. It was the beginning of a great career.

These days, Anne Paul Brinkman has stashed his overalls and wooden shoes in a closet. In his office next to his gallery in Barcelona, he receives clients who are just as enthusiastic as his very first shoppers, but who now come to ask him to create a sophisticated decor for them. Things do change.

How to define Brinkman's style? We perceive his Northern European origins immediately from his favorite colors—beige, sand, gray-blue, sage green—and his fondness for blond wood, stone, and black and white marble floors. Anne Paul Brinkman's Dutch heritage is no secret.

In Amsterdam, he received commissions to convert vacant former banks into apartments or veritable beehives of lofts. He was also asked to convert farms and hunting lodges into simulacra of cozy English country houses and to restore a ruined old Norman manor house that seemed to be in hopeless condition. Brinkman took on all

of these projects: he never shook off the decorating bug that bit him back when he was an antique dealer.

Brinkman is a disciple of the principle of *Gesamtkunstwerk* (total work of art). This concept dictates that the architect must design absolutely everything in a house: the furniture, the fabrics or papers that cover the walls, the decorative objects, the lighting, and even the door and window frames. Perhaps this inspired him to begin designing his own fabrics with motifs vaguely reminiscent of the organic forms of Art Nouveau. After the fabrics, he turned to lamps and wall fixtures, and then to lighting; he next took to tables, sofas, and armchairs. His designs became ubiquitous in the dwellings of the well-to-do: those magnificent period houses that line Amsterdam's canals, the luxurious apartments overlooking Central Park, and even the lobbies and bedrooms of boutique hotels.

Like many Dutch citizens, Anne Paul Brinkman loves to travel. After opening a store in the middle of New York's antique center, the Place des Antiquaires, he moved with his wife and children to two magnificent stately homes on the Keizersgracht in Amsterdam. And after his adventures back in the Netherlands, he moved on to the Costa Brava and Barcelona. Talent can voyage where it will, and everywhere it is greeted with open arms. Such is the experience of Anne Paul Brinkman, an exceptional talent from the North.

∗

295: Detail of a Chinoiserie-style wallpaper and a lacquered wood doorframe from the dining room of a château in Normandy. **296:** The oak table and high-backed chairs are Louis XIII, and the carpet is from the Savonnerie manufactory. The lacquered wood door was executed based on Brinkman's design. **297:** A large eighteenth-century Murano glass chandelier. The gilt bronze candelabrum dates from the reign of Napoleon III. **298–99:** The arabesques on this wallpaper designed by the architect harmonize with the ornate form of the fin-de-siècle candelabra. A nineteenth-century chandelier of gilt cast iron is reflected in the mirror. **300:** A neoclassical white marble bench decorated with griffons echoes the marble ornamentation in the entrance of this Amsterdam bank, now converted into a residence. **301:** In the former director's office, an armoire designed by the architect and a remarkable sculpted wood throne complement the warm tones of the paneling. **302:** On the top floor of a former office building in Amsterdam, Brinkman created a spacious loft. The white metal fireplace and the fabric on the nineteenth-century armchair also bear his signature, but the armchair to the right of the fireplace is a reissue of Charles Eames's famous Lounge Chair 670.

At Home with a Devotee
of Interior Design

Marie-Paule Pellé

Marie-Paule Pellé can boast of a truly international career. She left the mark of her unique vision and talent on the interior design magazines where she worked. The editor in chief of legendary publications such as *Décoration internationale* and *Vogue Décoration* prided herself—and this takes strength of character—on infallible judgment, energy to spare, and above all an insatiable curiosity. Over a good forty years, Marie-Paule Pellé has demonstrated that she has all these attributes. From the outset, she was an indefatigable spotter of antiques. She searched out firms and designers to produce her beloved "glossies." No object, no interior, and no talent escaped her voracious eye.

In the library of her charming nineteenth-century manor house, heaps of books she has produced and magazines she has managed are stacked on pedestal tables and even on the floor. Surprisingly, when it comes to her own residence she is rather reticent, even secretive. She would prefer that we sketch the portrait of a spacious Directoire family home with rose-hued render walls, gray-blue slatted shutters that Madeleine Castaing would have admired, and the delightful addition of an orangery.

Like all those who have traveled extensively, Marie-Paule Pellé has accumulated impressions and ideas. Her house reflects her warm personality. Open the door to the kitchen and take a seat on the big bench by the hearth to realize that the welcoming atmosphere is just a prologue to the visual surprises that await a guest.

We should mention that when Marie-Paule Pellé takes a fancy to richly brocaded silks, blue and white porcelain vases, French eighteenth-century portraits, or "witch balls," she collects them heedless of their quantity. No minimalism for this woman

with an insatiable appetite for lovely decorative objects, chairs covered with a surprising choice of fabrics, or an old plaster bust that she teasingly tops with a tricorn hat to lighten its lugubrious air. She is unfazed by exaggeration and pastiche and continually surprises with a dining room in the style of the flamboyant collector Carlos de Beistegui, a bedroom hung with *toile de Jouy* and furnished with a luxurious Indian bed, and a romantic guestroom that would be a perfect fit in George Sand's manor house.

Marie-Paule Pellé's greatest fear is the risk of becoming hostage to a style based exclusively on antique furnishings and objects. The "Pellé style" is not encapsulated by a pair of embroidered silk slippers tucked beneath an eighteenth-century bed with hangings *à la polonaise* or a lace fan artfully posed on a generously padded armchair. It is truly timeless and inspired by a curiosity about every era, every culture, and every style. It knows no bounds and certainly has future surprises in store for us.

*

305: In Pellé's bedroom, an ex-voto attached to a ribbon hangs on a wall covered with *toile de Jouy*.
306–7: A selection of Pellé's finds: porcelain vases and period furniture from a variety of eras, as well as an eighteenth-century copy of a portrait of Madame de Pompadour by François-Hubert Drouais.
308–9: A reproduction eighteenth-century fabric covers the walls and Louis XV *corbeille* sofa. On a Napoleon III blackamoor pedestal stands a candelabrum of Roman inspiration. **310:** The living room's lighthearted decor includes a Louis XV daybed upholstered in crimson silk damask. **311:** The dining room is an homage to Carlos de Beistegui and his famous dining room in the Château de Groussay.
312: Pellé found the Indian rosewood bed on one of her trips.

The White Tornado

Jan des Bouvrie

The Dutch decorator and designer Jan des Bouvrie is so fascinated by the color white that his compatriots have nicknamed him "the white tornado." Eschewing the slightest hint of color, des Bouvrie designs white houses with white interiors that spring from his prodigiously fertile imagination. He has given it free rein in residences in his native country, villas on the Côte d'Azur, and cottages tucked away in the groves of the Leeward Islands.

Jan des Bouvrie was born in 1940 in Naardenn, a peaceful little town north of Amsterdam. From his parents he inherited a consuming passion for contemporary design. In 1969, after concluding his studies at the renowned Rietveld Academy in Amsterdam, des Bouvrie experienced an immediate success with his design of a cube-shaped sofa covered in white fabric that he called "Kubus." From that point on, he was on the way to playing a leading role in the design world.

Jan des Bouvrie's career is a success story just as dazzling as his favorite color. Since the introduction of his Kubus, he can boast that he has converted his native land and a constantly growing international clientele to his ever-expanding empire of white. His honors now include an impressive array of individual designs, collections created for major firms, decorative schemes for private clients and hotel chains, the publication of several books on his highly personal vision of the art of good living, the opening of several stores dedicated to interior design, a television program on lifestyles, and, last but not least, an academy that bears his name.

The designer and his wife, the former model and stylist Monique des Bouvrie, live in a white villa in the heart of the Dutch countryside. They inhabit, needless to say, a white interior that serves as a backdrop for their collection of contemporary Chinese art. They also have a white villa on the Côte d'Azur and a very charming luxury getaway—all in white—in Curacao, overlooking the Caribbean.

If you want to live by des Bouvrie's mantra, you have to choose a spot that reflects your own personality. According to des Bouvrie, this setting is synonymous with a white Belle Epoque villa on the hills above Saint-Tropez, complete with a jade-colored swimming pool and a terrace shaded by towering palm trees, or perhaps a wooden house on a rocky peak whose gazebo overlooks the tranquil waters of the Lesser Antilles. A fantasy? No doubt. But most of us might dream of inhabiting the perfect house decorated by the white tornado from the North, its French doors flung wide open, its white curtains billowing in the breeze, its soft sofas covered in smooth white leather, with a glass of white wine in hand.

*

315: The des Bouvries' white house is built on a sheer rock. 316–17: Aside from *Tulipes* painted by the Dutch artist Jan Cremer, everything in the villa is of des Bouvrie's design. 318: In the living room, the ubiquitous whiteness creates a futuristic aura. 319: Monique's boudoir-dressing room has blue lighting installed at floor level. The white leather ottoman was designed by her husband. 320: A shallow alcove in the wall frames the king-size bed. The indirect lighting along the sides of the room creates the illusion of a blue sky.

Living in a Berlin Loft

Stefan Schad

The young German decorator Stefan Schad swears by contemporary design, Day-Glo colors, and sophisticated lighting. His clients willingly embrace his favorite combination of brilliant colors that "pop" against a blinding white background. Those who favor a subtle palette and a refined range of natural tones had best go elsewhere. For Schad, red means fire engine red, yellow means canary yellow, and green means apple green. His pinks and lavenders would not look out of place in the icing of tea cakes sold in Viennese coffee shops. His loft in Berlin is the best illustration imaginable of his obsession with overwhelming visual assaults on the senses.

Located on the fashionable Friedrichstrasse, the apartment building where he lives was constructed in 1899 in a hybrid style typical of the reign of Emperor Wilhelm II. Schad, a native of Hamburg but a Berliner at heart, fell in love with this sturdy red sandstone structure adorned with Venetian windows and topped with a glazed green tile Hansel and Gretel roof. When he walked into the mezzanine level, which once housed a dancing school, he was dazzled by the light-drenched space and decided on the spot to move in—the next day!

The enormous apartment on Friedrichstrasse has now become an homage to the great names of classic and contemporary design. Schad has brilliantly succeeded in arranging their creations side by side with exemplary subtlety. In the living room, a floor light by the Dutch designer Marcel Wanders for Moooi stands next to the legendary Ludwig Mies van der Rohe chaise longue, manufactured by Knoll, and the *Scala* light

from the Gunther Lambert collection. Elsewhere in the same room, Philippe Starck's *Lazy Working Sofa* is accompanied by a pair of *Archimoon* lamps distributed by Flos.

In contrast to what we might assume, Stefan Schad's decors do not resemble showroom catalogues, and although you may recognize famous names such as Eero Saarinen, Ray and Charles Eames, and Swarovski, Schad nevertheless manages to surprise us with the work of young designers, including Oliver Kesler and Günter Belzig.

The bedroom is usually the most intimate room in an apartment, house, or loft. Schad's is occupied by a round bed covered in white leather that he designed himself and a transparent *Bubble Chair* by Eero Aarnio. In addition, the white walls are lavishly hung with diaphanously sheer white curtains. A rather racy, ingeniously concealed lighting system can change the colors and ambiance of the room.

Berlin is a dynamic city with a distinctive vibe. The slender silhouettes of countless cranes are etched against the sky. The buildings that are going up are designed by the greatest architects of our time. Spectacular penthouses and lofts overlook breathtaking vistas. For innovative talents like Stefan Schad, creativity knows no bounds.

✳

323: In the hall leading to the bedroom, a Charles Eames chair stands by the window. **324–25:** In his living room, Stefan Schad has assembled an array of his favorite designs: the *Big Shadow* lamp by Marcel Wanders, Ludwig Mies van der Rohe's chaise longue, Pierre Paulin's *Tongue No. 577* chair, and Philippe Starcks's *Lazy Working Sofa* and *Super Archimoon* lamp. **326–27:** With the aid of an ingenious lighting system, Schad can vary the color of his bedroom. The hanging *Bubble Chair* is by Eero Aarnio. **328:** The ceramic red crosses arranged on the Altuglas shelf in the kitchen are simply salt and pepper shakers!

From Haute Couture
to Interior Decoration

Pierre Yovanovitch

He began designing men's collections for Pierre Cardin at a young age. After working there for eight years, Pierre Yovanovitch decided to bid farewell to haute couture and devote himself entirely to his true and unique passion: interior decoration.

He was immediately successful. As soon as he completed work on the apartments of several friends, commissions began to pour in. Yovanovitch recalls that he was surprised by this rapid rise to prominence because his style is austerely spare and appeals only to those who share his aversion to needlessly cluttered interiors, experiencing visual nausea when confronted with examples of the "more is more" aesthetic.

Pierre Yovanovitch has a strong predilection for spotless white, natural tones, oak, marble, contemporary art, and the work of great twentieth-century American designers.

When he moved into a huge apartment with a panoramic view over the Place de la Concorde, Yovanovitch decided that his new home would be the essence of visual serenity. There would be no clutter in these generously proportioned rooms—only unfinished wood floors, a bathroom of schist, pale wood wall paneling, armchairs and sofas of his own design, and artworks signed by Georg Baselitz, Alex Katz, Marc Quinn, and Francesco Clemente.

Like all creative minds, Pierre Yovanovitch is endlessly on a quest for fresh ideas. His curiosity is boundless, and with each project, he pursues new forms and new technical possibilities. He seeks out furniture, lighting, decorative objects, and color that will combine to make every project a new sensation, whether in a sturdy sixteenth-century stone house tucked away like a jealously guarded secret in the heart of Provence, a group

of restaurants in one of the skyscrapers of Paris's La Défense, or in a spectacularly proportioned apartment at one the capital's most sought after addresses along the Seine. The American magazine *Architectural Digest* named Yovanovitch as the only French decorator in its most recent "100 Top Talents in Architecture + Interior Design" list. He has the ability to continually call everything into question and create interiors that are just as fresh as his earliest work.

Pierre Yovanovitch's designs are resolutely cotemporary, yet timeless. Precise and meticulous down to the last detail, sometimes enhanced with lighting fixtures and coffee tables of his own design, these interiors are haute couture creations with the undeniable elegance and chic of a well-tailored suit. At heart, Pierre Yovanovitch never really left the world of masculine style. Instead of wielding fine fabrics and scissors, he creates beauty with colors, forms, and light combined into a flawlessly tailored architectural ensemble.

*

331: From the small sitting room with walls paneled in pale wood, there is a view of the living room and a painting by Alex Katz. **332–33:** A magnificent canvas by Georg Baselitz dominates the living room. The furnishings were designed by the master of the house. **334:** In the living room, a painting by Marc Quinn hangs above the mantelpiece. The sofas enveloped in wood are the decorator's design. **335:** Detail of the austerely furnished dining room. **336:** In the bedroom, which is entirely paneled in pale wood, the built-in bed is mounted on a raised platform. **337:** A narrow band of light twists around the spiral staircase, subtly illuminating the steps. Throughout the entire apartment—from the corridor leading to the bathroom to the intimate little sitting room—blond tonalities of natural wood predominate. **338:** A photograph signed by Sam Samore hangs on the rear wall of the kitchen designed by Yovanovitch.

American Chic

Stephen Sills

Stephen Sills was born in Oklahoma, and he retains the local drawl and affection for verdant landscapes that stretch as far as the eye can see. But his consuming passion for decoration could only come to fruition in New York. From early days, it was clear that this little boy who was always decorating and redecorating his parents' house was destined to flourish in the Big Apple.

Stephen Sills, now Manhattan's most visible designer, has celebrities like Tina Turner, Vera Wang, and Anna Wintour among his clients. The idol of senior editors of shelter magazines and the author of several books on his very personal vision of how to decorate a home, he also lent his signature style to the transformation of hotels, including the Connaught in London and the St. Regis in New York. He was recently commissioned to give a new look to the Apthorp, a white elephant of an apartment building in the Renaissance Revival style on Manhattan's Upper West Side, built between 1906 and 1908 for William Waldorf Astor. The asking price per square foot for a condominium here is around 6,000 US dollars!

When it comes to interior decoration, most Americans insist on a flawless finish. They may admire a *mas* in Provence, a picturesque old farmhouse with flaking wooden shutters and lichen-covered roofs, or a Burgundian manor house that bears the patina of centuries. But when it comes to their own homes, they expect nothing less than absolute perfection. Stephen Sills is familiar with every nuance of the demands of his celebrity clients. However, in his country house in Westchester County, which Karl Lagerfeld has described as the chicest house in America, he opted for a relaxed

atmosphere, a look that is more sports shirt than button-down collar. This house, with its pristine New England look, is graced with the finest antique furnishings and major works of contemporary art, but the tone is one of studied nonchalance with the refined negligence of old European homes.

Located in Bedford, near other extensive estates, Sills's retreat is secluded in a property planted with century-old trees and a *parc à l'anglaise*, a romantic feat of landscape engineering that seems to be a precise replication of Albion's beloved countryside. Within, there is a perfect harmony between simple architecture and rustic accents, including Sills's lucky finds gleaned from the four corners of the world. Walls have been given an old world patina or are covered with distressed stucco to serve as a backdrop for Italian, Russian, and French eighteenth- and nineteenth-century furniture, a pair of sixteenth-century Turkish columns, a plaster hanging light fixture by Giacometti, and artworks signed by Pablo Picasso, Cy Twombly, and Jean Arp.

Stephen Sills is the uncontested master of bold juxtaposition. He has a unique ability to juggle risky combinations. Watch him wend his way among Paris antiques dealers or London auction houses if you want to learn how he manages to combine Regency armchairs with a fragment of ancient marble, or a painting by Rauschenberg with a pair of Chinese faience stools.

Always on the quest for beauty, the decorator has a boundless sense of enthusiasm. Today he might be in New York, tomorrow in the heart of the Parisian neighborhood around Boulevard Saint-Germain. A couple of months later, he might turn up in the back room of a store in London's trendy Pimlico. Wherever you cross his path, you can be sure that Sills is en route to finding fresh novelties for our aesthetic delectation.

*

341: The seats on either side of the Scottish red marble fireplace are from the Tsarskoïe Selo Palace. **342:** A corner in the dining room. The sculpture is by Jean Arp and the drawings are signed by Joan Miró. **343:** The sofa is of Sills's design and the picture hung above is a work by Robert Rauschenberg. **344:** In the guesthouse, the floor is stone. The cabriolet chairs are Louis XV. **345:** The stairwell walls are covered with bleached chestnut panels. The pastel is by Picasso. **346:** The marble base is an eighteenth-century copy of a Roman original. **347:** A felt sculpture by Robert Morris hangs in the guesthouse. **348–49:** The house is set in a lovely park filled with wildlife sculptures that date from the nineteenth century. **350:** In the library, an eighteenth-century marble bust is posed on a wooden pedestal of the same period.